Doing Theology in the Age of Trump

WESTAR SEMINAR ON GOD AND THE HUMAN FUTURE

The Westar Seminar on God and the Human Future stays true to Westar's dual mission of (1) conducting collaborative, cumulative research in the academic study of religion, and (2) promoting religious literacy in public discourse. The Seminar on God and the Human Future emerges from the academic fields of Philosophy of Religion, Critical Theory, and Radical Theology. The Seminar seeks to reimagine the concept of God and the value of religion in the 21st century. All publications arising from the Seminar that are placed in this series aim to invoke dialogue and participation in the task of addressing critical issues in religion today.

Doing Theology in the Age of Trump

A Critical Report on Christian Nationalism

EDITED BY *Jeffrey W. Robbins*
and Clayton Crockett

CASCADE *Books* · Eugene, Oregon

DOING THEOLOGY IN THE AGE OF TRUMP
A Critical Report on Christian Nationalism

Westar Seminar on God and the Human Future

Cascade Books
An Imprint of Wipf and Stock Publishers
199 W. 8th Ave., Suite 3
Eugene, OR 97401

www.wipfandstock.com

PAPERBACK ISBN: 978-1-5326-0886-5
HARDCOVER ISBN: 978-1-5326-0887-2
EBOOK ISBN: 978-1-5326-0888-9

Cataloging-in-Publication data:

Names: Robbins, Jeffrey W., editor. | Crockett, Clayton, editor.

Title: Doing theology in the age of Trump : a critical report on Christian nationalism / edited by Jeffrey W. Robbins and Clayton Crockett.

Description: Eugene, OR: Cascade Books, 2018. | Weststar Seminar on God and the Human Future.| Includes bibliographical references.

Identifiers: ISBN: 978-1-5326-0886-5 (PAPERBACK). | ISBN: 978-1-5326-0887-2 (HARDCOVER). | ISBN: 978-1-5326-0888-9 (EBOOK).

Subjects: LCSH: Trump, Donald, 1946—Influence. | Nationalism—Religious aspects—Christianity. | Religious right—United States—History—21st century. | Christianity and politics—United States—History—21st century.

Classification: BR516 D64 2018 (print). | BR516 D64 (epub).

Manufactured in the U.S.A.   NOVEMBER 6, 2018

Contents

CONTENTS

Contributors

Joe Bessler is the Robert Travis Peake Professor of Theology at Phillips Theological Seminary. Author of *A Scandalous Jesus: How Three Historic Quests Changed Theology for the Better*, he is currently at work on a project, tentatively titled *Moving Words: How Theology Proposes to Lead beyond God*.

Karen Bray is an Assistant Professor of Religion and Philosophy, and the chair of Religious Studies and Philosophy, at Wesleyan College. Her research areas include continental philosophy of religion; feminist, critical disability, black studies, queer, political, and decolonial theories and theologies; and secularism and the postsecular. She is particularly interested in exploring how secular institutions and cultures behave theologically.

Sarah Morice Brubaker is Associate Professor of Theology at Phillips Theological Seminary, the program unit chair for the Liberal Theologies Group of the American Academy of Religion, and a Westar Institute fellow. Her book, *The Place of the Spirit*, was published in 2013 by Wipf and Stock.

John D. Caputo, the Thomas J. Watson Professor of Religion Emeritus (Syracuse University) and the David R. Cook Professor of Philosophy Emeritus (Villanova University) is a constructive theologian who works in the area of radical theology. His most recent work includes *Truth* (2013), *The Folly of God* (2015), and *Hermeneutics: Facts and Interpretation in the Age of Information* (2018). Keith Putt edited *A Caputo Reader* (2018), a collection of his work from the early 1970s to the present. His *A Radical Theology of the Cross* will be forthcoming in 2019, and a second edition of *On Religion* in the fall of 2018.

CONTRIBUTORS

Clayton Crockett is Professor and Director of Religious Studies at the University of Central Arkansas. He is the author of *Radical Political Theology* and *Derrida after the End of Writing,* among other books. He is an editor, along with Creston Davis, Jeffrey W. Robbins, and Slavoj Žižek, of the book series "Insurrections: Critical Studies in Religion, Politics, and Culture."

David Galston is the Executive Director of the Westar Institute and the Ecumenical Chaplain at Brock University in St. Catharines, Ontario, where he is also an Adjunct Professor of Philosophy. A Fellow of the Jesus Seminar and a United Church minister, David has led many workshops across Canada and the United States on the question of the historical Jesus, the future of Christianity, and the problems of Christian theology in light of the historical Jesus. He is the author of *God's Human Future* (2016), *Embracing the Human Jesus* (2012), and *Archives and the Event of God* (2011).

James Howard Hill Jr. is a PhD student in the areas of Religious Studies and African American Studies at Northwestern University. Hill works in the areas of Black studies, cultural studies, critical religious studies, performance studies, and theology.

Michael S. Hogue is Professor of Theology, Ethics and Philosophy of Religion at Meadville Lombard Theological School (Chicago). He is the author, most recently, of *American Immanence: Democracy for an Uncertain World* (Insurrections, 2018). His teaching and scholarship explore the intersections among religion, politics, and the environment.

Catherine Keller is George T. Cobb Professor of Constructive Theology in the Graduate Division of Religion of Drew University. Books she has authored include *From a Broken Web: Separation, Sexism and Self; Apocalypse Now & Then; God & Power; Face of the Deep: A Theology of Becoming; On the Mystery: Discerning God in Process; Cloud of the Impossible: Negative Theology and Planetary Entanglement;* and *Intercarnations: Exercises in Theological Possibility.* Her most recent book is *Political Theology of the Earth: Our Planetary Emergency and the Struggle for a New Public.*

Rev. Dr. **Robin R. Meyers** is senior minister of Mayflower Congregational UCC church of Oklahoma City and Distinguished Professor Emeritus in the Philosophy Department at Oklahoma City University. His most recent book is *Spiritual Defiance: Building a Beloved Community of Resistance*, and forthcoming: *Falling Off the Ceiling: The Death of Michelangelo's God and the Rebirth of Wonder*.

Daniel Miller is Associate Professor of Religion and Social Thought in the Department of Liberal Studies at Landmark College. His research focuses on the intersections of political theory, religion, and secularism. His first book was *The Myth of Normative Secularism: Religion and Politics in the Democratic Homeworld* (2016).

Jordan E. Miller is a community organizer, interdisciplinary teacher, and scholar who specializes in religion, social movements, and resistance studies. His first monograph, *Resisting Theology, Furious Hope*, includes chapters on The AIDS Coalition to Unleash Power (ACT UP), Occupy Wall Street, and #BlackLivesMatter. He is the editor of *The Palgrave Handbook of Radical Theology* with Christopher D. Rodkey.

Hollis Phelps is an assistant professor of interdisciplinary studies at Mercer University. He is the author of *Alain Badiou: Between Theology and Anti-Theology* and co-editor (with Philip Goodchild) of *Religion and European Philosophy: Key Thinkers from Kant to Žižek*. His current research focuses on the theological, moral, social, political, and economic valences of debt.

Alan Jay Richard is an independent scholar and religious organizer associated with Realistic Living, a nonprofit organization located in rural north Texas with the mission of encouraging new forms of religious life. As part of this effort, he serves on the board of the local environmental nonprofit Citizens United for Resources and Environment, organizes resistance to corporate environmental devastation in rural sacrifice zones, participates in local and regional direct action efforts, and lectures on topics related to politics, religious change, and inter-religious dialogue. His current scholarly interests include political ecclesiology and the religious aspects of American popular culture.

Jeffrey W. Robbins is Professor of Religion and Philosophy at Lebanon Valley College, where he also serves as the director of the American Studies program and the Undergraduate Research Symposium, and as the Faculty Mentor for the Allwein Scholars Program. He is a member of the Board of

Directors and is a Research Fellow for the Westar Institute where he chairs the ongoing collaborative academic seminar on God and the Human Future. He is the author or editor of nine books, including most recently *Radical Theology: A Vision for Change* (2016), and co-author of *An Insurrectionist Manifesto: Four New Gospels for a Radical Politics* (2016), which was named as a Choice Outstanding Academic Title in 2016. He is also a contributing editor of the *Journal for Cultural and Religious Theory* and co-editor of the book series "Insurrections: Critical Studies in Religion, Politics, and Culture."

Mark Lewis Taylor is Professor of Theology and Culture at Princeton Theological Seminary. Most relevant to his essay in this volume are his recent books *The Executed God: The Way of the Cross in Lockdown American* (2nd ed., 2016), *The Theological and the Political: On the Weight of the World* (2011), and *Religion, Politics and the Christian Right: Post 9/11 Powers and American Empire* (2005).

Noëlle Vahanian is Professor of Philosophy at Lebanon Valley College, in Annville, Pennsylvania, where she teaches courses on genocide, world philosophies, and philosophy of religion. She is the author of *Language, Desire, and Theology: A Genealogy of the Will to Speak* (2003), *The Rebellious No: Variations on a Secular Theology of Language* (2014), and most recently the co-author of *An Insurrectionist Manifesto: Four New Gospels for a Radical Politics* (2016).

Introduction

Doing Theology in the Age of Trump

JEFFREY W. ROBBINS AND CLAYTON CROCKETT

One may legitimately ask what *theology* has to do with Donald Trump. Or, more precisely, what theology might contribute to a growing chorus of critics of President Trump and more broadly whatever might go by the name of the nationalist populist movement we are calling Trumpism. Let there be no doubt—we completely repudiate not only the administration of Trump but also the white Christian nationalism that it represents.

At the same time, given the multitude of repudiating voices, the question can be raised: is this book meant merely as an act of catharsis, some kind of emotional discharge, or some kind of effort to distance or relieve ourselves of a collective sense of complicity? Put in more religious terms, is this our purchase on indulgences—at once to acknowledge our guilt, to accept blame, and to recognize that our current political crisis and fractured state of society are the fate of our own making, while we simultaneously beg for pardon?

Alternatively, does this book merely pile on as the flaws in Trump's character and competence as a leader have been exposed? As the various journalistic efforts to chronicle the dysfunction within the White House and the contradictions within Trumpism as a movement mount, what if anything does a critical theological sensibility bring to the equation? Are we late to the party? Are we redundant, or at the very least, derivative?

If the answer to any of the questions above is yes, then it is our view that our efforts have been wasted. It is clear that theology no longer operates as the "queen of the sciences" as it once did in the late Middle Ages when the authority of the church in the Christian West was at its height, and that it no longer speaks in a unified voice as was the dream and promise of Christian orthodoxy. Long past are the days when any priestly or papal authority prerogative to speak on behalf of the church universal is accepted by the world's faithful Christians or all practicing churches. At least since the time of the Protestant Reformation, the ability and right of the church to stamp out dissent and enforce conformity have proven to be a fool's dream—even worse, a dangerous delusion that betrays a violent tendency. If theology operates without a unified authority, if it is incapable to unify and powerless to compel obedience, then what exactly is its point?

Before we take this question up directly, it is important for us also to say a word about resistance. At its most basic, resistance stands opposed to power. But both resistance and power must be complexified. Neither are as simple and straightforward as they appear. For instance, perhaps the single greatest allure of power is that it is able to enact its will. And while the quip is that absolute power corrupts absolutely, individuals, institutions, and movements nevertheless quest it, for it holds out the promise of a seamless realization of one's wishes, dreams, and visions. So conceived, the effort to remove any friction or opposition is the most efficient way to maximize power and thus actualize one's will.

But the great lesson from Michel Foucault, which has been advanced by a great number of contemporary philosophers, social critics, and cultural theorists, is that wherever there is power, there is also resistance. Further, the greater the power, the greater the resistance. In this way, resistance is not only a counter to power, but actually exists as a counterpower. And while never simple or straightforward, this definition of resistance must be understood quite literally. As a counter to power, resistance as a counterpower operates in a fashion otherwise than power. It does not simply oppose power with power but offers an alternative to power traditionally conceived.

One way that resistance can be understood as an alternative to power is by thinking in terms of *intersectionality*. Kimberlé Williams Crenshaw was the first to use this term. She is a civil rights advocate, legal scholar, and critical race theorist. The idea is that our politics and related social justice efforts should be overlapping and multiform because our social identities are overlapping and multiform. Categories such as race, gender, class, and sexual orientation cannot be thought in isolation. There are gradations of

power and privilege, and conversely gradations of bias, discrimination, oppression, and subjugation. The politics of identity that pits the particular
situation or grievances of one specific group over against another must
be more broadly construed so that a genuine coalition of interests can be
discerned and formed. This is not the reduction of differences to the least
common denominator, or a "big-tent" approach to political organizing; on
the contrary, it is a recognition of how the various forms of oppression
interrelate to contribute to a vast, dynamic, and seeming impenetrable network of systemic injustice and marginalization.[1]

The point of this in relation to resistance is that it rejects an all-or-
nothing approach. The counter to power takes many forms. This plurivocal
and multiform nature of resistance is not a sign of its weakness but the
means by which resistance may operate as a genuine counterpower. What
excites us most by this prospect is that politics need not be played as a
zero-sum game with a winner-take-all mentality. As the chapters that follow demonstrate, resistance to Trump and to Christian nationalism is not
simply reactive, but releases generative and vital agonisms that infuse life
into our socius.

Part 1 focuses more explicitly on these broader issues of Christian
nationalism. Robin Meyers poses the basic question, "Is God a Christian
nationalist?" In chapters 2 and 3, Alan Richard and Sarah Morice Brubaker
investigate some more historical background and context for contemporary expressions of white Christian nationalism. James Howard Hill
Jr. demonstrates in chapter 4 how insufficient are protests solely against
Donald Trump and Trumpism, because they belie a situation of insidious
privileges and racial and racist assumptions. For Jeffrey W. Robbins, Karen
Bray, and Clayton Crockett, truly grappling with the entrenchment of white
Christian nationalism in the United States means coming to terms with
its pervasiveness and our own implication and involvement in it. In the
concluding chapter of part 1, Mark Lewis Taylor outlines some strategies
for theological resistance to this oppressive and wide-ranging Christian
nationalism.

In many respects the entire book engages with various aspects of
Christian nationalism, but the chapters in part 2 reach beyond this nationalism narrowly circumscribed, to take up questions of American exceptionalism, the situation of contemporary Christian evangelicalism, and
finally the strange and brutal phenomenon of Trumpism itself. John D.

1. Crenshaw, "Kimberlé Crenshaw on intersectionality."

INTRODUCTION

Caputo offers a scathing critique of what passes for Christianity in the U.S. in chapter 9, and calls for a prophetic spirit to animate our resistance and for us to imagine the possibility of an America to come. Michael Hogue shows how American exceptionalism culminates in Donald Trump, and Catherine Keller explains in chapter 11 how evangelicals have degenerated into "Foxangelicals," people more animated by their hatred of others—liberals, gays, multiculturalists, immigrants, and terrorists—than by any real commitment to biblical Christianity. According to Daniel Miller, we cannot expect white American evangelicals to change; any significant transformation must come from without. In chapter 13, Jordan E. Miller and Hollis Phelps demonstrate how Trumpism has become more a state of affairs than a state of emergency or exception, and Joe Bessler confronts Trump with the extraordinary novel by Nobel laureate Toni Morrison, *Beloved*, in chapter 14. David Galston ties Trumpism and contemporary Christianity to the movement of postmodernism, and finally in the last chapter Noëlle Vahanian gives us a profound meditation on the nature of history and fiction that goes to the heart of our sense of identity.

What these various examples prove is that resistance is not reactive, but constitutive. It is generative and regenerative. It opens new pathways, discloses different possibilities. Put otherwise, resistance is not a negative power but an affirmative one. This is made clear by Naomi Klein in the excellent book she wrote in the immediate aftermath of the Trump election and inauguration: *No Is Not Enough: Resisting Trump's Shock Politics and Winning the World We Need*. While the book was at least partly a relitigation of the campaign—in terms of Hillary Clinton's failed strategy; Democratic Party infighting; Trump's false promises; and inflamed racial tension, xenophobia, and sexism, and so forth—and partly an analysis and condemnation of Trumpism in line with Klein's well-known theory of the "shock doctrine," more fundamentally *No Is Not Enough* is an articulation of the various ways groups large and small are mobilized and rallying around cherished values suddenly under threat, hard-earned policy advances, and a whole pandemonium of visions for the future worth fighting for. What has become increasingly clear is that the demands of the climate warriors, while distinct, are not at odds with several millions who showed up for the Women's March one day after Trump's inauguration. Likewise, while much was made of the electoral success of Trump due to his appeal to largely white, blue-collar workers in the industrial Northeast and Midwest, the noncorporatist progressive economic policies argued for by the left are good for white and African American workers alike. So while the tendency and temptation is to condemn Trump and Trumpism, it is not a winning strategy if it fails to articulate something positive we can believe in.

Further Klein makes the case that one of the most important lessons we can learn from the Trump election is that especially in this time of crisis, disillusionment, and grievance, the radical is also ironically the pragmatic. With the widespread distrust of the establishment—whether they be party insiders, career politicians, or the mainstream media—the population is open to revolutionary change. By his tweets and his one-time alliance with Steve Bannon, Trump has been able to fashion himself as the great disrupter. While this might quell the populist rage, when one more closely examines his actual policies and the legislation that has passed under his watch, he has actually proven to be a traditional conservative further entrenching a neoliberal corporate agenda. Meanwhile, offering up something truly new and different are the movements #BlackLivesMatter and #MeToo on a large scale, and on a smaller scale a group led by nuns in their eighties and nineties, from the Order of the Catholic Sisters of the Adorers of the Blood of Christ, fighting for climate justice.

Here we might remake the link with theology—and more specifically might rethink what theology might contribute to what is already a strong, vocal, and varied anti-Trump movement, a veritable wave of resistance? This collection of essays is a product of the Westar Institute's academic seminar on God and the Human Future. The God Seminar, as it is commonly known, began its work in 2013. It takes its lead from the pioneering research and public notice of the Jesus Seminar, of the prior generation. In a short time, it has attracted over thirty participating Research Fellows who together are exploring new ways of and new images for thinking about God in a posttheistic context.

Unlike the past academic seminars of the Westar Institute, the God Seminar consists primarily of philosophers of religion, critical theorists, and radical theologians, rather than biblical scholars and historians. But what it shares in common with previous seminars is the twofold mission of Westar—namely, to conduct collaborative, cumulative research on controversial topics that advance the academic study of religion, and to equip the general public with tools to critically evaluate competing claims in the public discussion of religion. We are not bound by Christian orthodoxy or ecclesiastical authority. We bring a critical sensibility to our study of religion and our theological thinking. We have been greatly informed and are deeply indebted to the pioneering research and landmark publications of the academic seminars on Jesus, Paul, and the Acts of the Apostles that have offered an entire paradigm shift for how we see the origins of Christianity in its proper historical context as specifically an anti-imperial movement. And so, we are attuned to the violent normalcy of worldly power. We have been made aware of how often the power of the state presents itself as a rival religion. We believe that nationalistic, patriotic fervor easily and often devolves into idolatry, and when it does, that it is important for us to identify it as fundamentally anti-Christian, if indeed there is such a thing as Christianity in any integral way. Even further, one of the things that unites us in our ongoing collaborative research endeavor is the conviction that this political opposition to a form of worldly power oriented around military might, domination, and denigration is actually the way of Jesus. How else ought we to understand Jesus's death sentence and eventual crucifixion as an enemy of the state?

Many of the essays included in this volume address the ways the Trump campaign successfully in attracting over 80 percent of the Christian evangelical vote. Much of the discussion of this within the media has portrayed evangelical support for Trump as either a contradiction or a compromising of the values and convictions of evangelicalism. What we show, however, is that this evangelical support for Trump is neither a contradiction nor a compromise of the spiritual integrity of the Religious Right; instead, the argument is made that Trump—or more precisely, Trumpism, in all its populist, nationalist, white male rage—is the culmination and actualization of Christian evangelicalism. *Trump is not the exception, but the rule.* While we may be shocked by the bullying and by the personal insults he hurls on Twitter and the myriad ways he defies convention, undermines the public trust, attacks the free press, and so on, the fact that he has successfully tapped into white Christian grievance, Islamophobia, and misogyny should not surprise anyone paying attention to the cultural trends and wholesale political realignment that has taken place at least since the time of Nixon's famed Southern Strategy.

Democrats supported the Civil Rights bill of 1964 after John F. Kennedy's assassination in the context of Lyndon B. Johnson's attempt to promote a Great Society despite his inability to stop the expansion of the war in Vietnam. This political shift opened up an opportunity for Republicans to appeal to disenchanted white Southerners who were alienated and frightened by the radical implications of desegregation. Over the course of the next three decades, with some brief counterinstances under Jimmy Carter and Bill Clinton, Republicans consolidated their hold on the American South. Racism was more latent but persisted just beneath the surface, just as it was part of the war on drugs and the dramatic expansion of incarceration. As the Christian Right emerged onto the political scene in the 1980s, its appeal to conservative religious and theological issues masked much of the underlying racism.

The racism of disaffected whites and the preoccupation of conservative Christians with cultural values were and are two sides of the same coin. When the religious element of Republican politics was more evident, its racial element was less obvious. But when the political influence of Christian conservatives peaked in the 2004 reelection of George W. Bush, it went underground in the wake of a more secular and at the time atheistic backlash. Bush lost the support of most of the country with his response to the Hurricane Katrina disaster, and Barack Obama was elected by a populace surging with hope for change. Under Obama, the cultural conservatives regrouped as the Tea Party, which channeled explicitly economic anxiety and served as a repository for racist reactions to Obama's presidency.

During Obama's presidency, religion became less evident, as racial and cultural issues became more prominent. The manifestation of white racism as fear and loathing of Obama and Obamacare canalized rural economic insecurity. Trump "won" by appealing to this lowest common denominator: this fear of the "others" (blacks, immigrants, Muslims, liberals, radicals) who were responsible for stealing "our" country and its wealth—the country and the wealth of whites, of blue-collar workers, of conservatives, of God-loving Americans. The incredible support of conservative evangelical Christians who voted for Trump despite any indication that Trump himself is personally pious or evangelical indicates how deeply aligned white racism and racialism and white Christianity in fact are.

But the fact that evangelicalism is the most audible theological voice within the American public *does not mean* that it exhausts the theological possibilities or critical religious resources available to us. By identifying with the tradition of radical theology, the God Seminar is hoping to provide a theological analogue to Klein's *No Is Not Enough*. While radical theology might have first come to public notice in Friedrich Nietzsche's proclamation of the death of God in the work of Thomas J. J. Altizer, William Hamilton, and others, even more fundamental to both Nietzsche and radical theology is the affirmation of life and its value in the face of the state, empire, or sovereign that claims the right to deliver us to death. This affirmative sensibility is what drives the prophetic indignation at the idols and perverse worship of worldly power. It is also this affirmative theological sensibility that makes our political engagement in worldly affairs our permanent responsibility. There can be no radical theology that is not simultaneously a political theology.

What follows is a series of essays that offer a rival, oppositional, alternative political theology to that of the white, Christian nationalist political theology of Trump and Trumpism. Godspeed to the resistance.

PART 1

History, Race, and Christian Nationalism in America

1

Is God a Christian Nationalist?

ROBIN MEYERS

The rhetorician Kenneth Burke is best known for his theories of human communication as drama. But perhaps his most famous quote is about the essence of the human species itself. This is pre–inclusive language, but otherwise it's a masterpiece: *Man is the symbol-using (symbol-making, symbol-misusing) animal, inventor of the negative, separated from his natural condition by instruments of his own making, goaded by the spirit of hierarchy, and rotten with perfection.*[1]

You may wonder what this has to do with Trump and the rise of Christian nationalism, but let's begin with our capacity to make symbols, use symbols, and misuse symbols. Only human beings create *signifiers* that stand for something else, which is not the same thing as the thing signified, but which invariably becomes confused with it—and then, in some cases, inseparable from it. This is especially true when the symbol is an image. Consider one of the most universal symbols in the world, the red cursive script that says Coca-Cola. Upon seeing it, people who like Coke can have a visceral response to the symbol, especially if they are thirsty. Coke was once referred to as the "real thing"—which is odd given that it is an artificially colored, artificially flavored, artificially carbonated nonnutritional beverage partaking of absolutely nothing real. But this does not matter. *The symbol has the power to become the thing it symbolizes,* and logic neither creates the effect nor negates it.

1. Burke, *Language as Symbolic Action*, 16.

Now consider the most iconic image of God in the Western world since the Renaissance, the portrait of God on the ceiling of the Sistine Chapel.

He is an older male, bearded but with a youthful body, and has the face of a European Elder. Is that Eve under his arm? Is she a present? What holds him up? Is he enclosed in some kind of heavenly drapery? Regardless, there is no mistaking his gender as he reaches out surrounded by angels, extending his hand to a reclining Adam, who is noticeably not working very hard at making contact.

Intellectually we know that it is "just a symbol," of course, and not the thing symbolized, but tell that to the heart. Existentially what is true of this image of God is also true of the iconic images of Santa Claus or Superman. When asked to explain or describe either one, the *original images remain*, as if a default setting in the brain. Our connotative responses to them are stamped on the psyche, stronger than any linguistic and conceptual explanations of the generous qualities of Santa Claus, for example, or the world-saving powers of Superman. Words are strong, but the image is stronger.

Research has shown that archetypal images, especially powerful and formative ones, are never fully removed as default settings in the brain until they are *replaced by different images*. So to use the civil rights movement as an example, it was the image of southern police officers turning the fire hoses on young protestors, and sending in the dogs, that displaced other images that white Americans had of African Americans as something other than the object of humiliation and violence.

Although many people will not, when asked to describe God, speak of God as an old, bearded, white Guy in the Sky, precious few other images replace the ones we have. Since images of God are by definition difficult to come by, the default image for God that remains in most people's minds, I would argue, is Michelangelo's depiction of Blake's nobodaddy. He is not only "up" there somewhere (which is a difficult concept itself, given that "up" is a relative concept when you live on a round planet), but He is clearly the King of the Universe (there are no other gods around him), and he's white, and the man he is reaching down to help is white, and the heavenly hosts that surround him are all white. This is not just white male privilege at the top of the food chain, but Cosmic White Privilege at the top of the Cosmic Food Chain. He is not, after all, reaching down to bless a woman, or a child of color, or even an animal.

The gap between God's finger and Adam's finger is one way to understand Burke's phrase, *inventor of the negative* and *goaded by hierarchy*. We know what we are—humans—because we know what we are not—God. And although we try to draw near, we will never finally leave our place in the scheme of things. What's more, although we want to be like God, because we are *rotten with perfection* and always striving, separation is the fundamental human condition.

When we look at what is happening in American politics today, I would argue that we are experiencing, in Trump's rise to power, a psychosexual backlash to the default setting of the white cosmic hierarchy represented by Michelangelo's depiction of God. After eight years of a *black* man in the *White* House, and facing the prospect of eight more years of a woman (who wore pants no less) becoming the default leader of the American family, the rise of Christian nationalism, while attributable to many factors, is also fundamentally grounded in what many white males of all social classes perceive to be the need for a kind of *emergency reset* of the pecking order of reality itself—a restoration of the maleness of God, the whiteness of God, the straightness of God, and the in-charge resoluteness of God.

What's more, in Michelangelo's image of a God reaching down to connect with a creature that he has created but that he also seems to have lost control of, many disaffected and struggling white males see a metaphor for all displaced fathers who reach out to reel in those who need to reassert control of their families, their authority, and their (white, male, straight, authoritarian) hegemony.

As an older white male, I can easily go undercover in Oklahoma City while wearing work clothes and a baseball cap in Home Depot. Trump voters will talk to me because they think I am one of them. What they tell me is that the world they once knew has unraveled and is threatened by idiots (liberals, professors, government bureaucrats, uppity women, welfare blacks, and those forcing a "gay agenda" on the world). It may be a twisted way to use Burke, but they are very much "goaded by hierarchy." They believe that suddenly *nobody knows their place*, much less stays in it.

What's more, Michelangelo's heterosexual God (created by a homosexual artist) has the right, so our scriptures tell us (Gen 6:1–4), to take (to sexually assault) the "daughters of the earth." This is the Harvey Weinstein of heaven. God's famous "reach" as depicted by Michelangelo is not in this case to a daughter of the earth but to his "son." The gesture appears like a kind of cosmic "bromance"—extending the White Father's divine hand to the white prodigal son's reluctant hand, as if to say, "Come home, bubba." Get up, be a man, lead the household of the earth, and subdue it, and do not succumb to your emasculation at the hands of those who would displace you, who would dethrone you, who would render you superfluous in a world of lesbians and artificial insemination. I have a real woman for you under my arm, a "helper" made from your spare rib.

While right-wing nationalists were marching in Poland last week, they kept chanting, "We want God!" Trump used the same phrase, and it was his biggest applause line.[2] The question is, what God is everyone talking about here? We know the answer, because we have a default image of God in the West, not yet replaced by a new image, and Trump is, not surprisingly, the earthly mirror of that image for the most disaffected among us: Son of Sky God. Call it a frightening twist on the incarnation.

Trump also lives in a gilded world, in gaudy palaces, surrounded by earthly angels (supermodels) and is, like his father, appropriately jealous, short-tempered, impetuous, and insulting when the times call for Daddy to throw a fit in the house by "tweeting others as he would not want to be tweeted." We are indeed, as Burke put it, *separated from [our] natural condition by instruments of [our] own making.* Son of Nobodaddy uses his cell phone to send thunderbolts in the middle of the night.

He comes to cast the evil ones out of the garden for the sin of not obeying him (drain the swamp), to keep the brown ones at bay (build a wall), and to Make America White Again. He would leave black college basketball players in jail in China for not properly adoring him, while excusing Roy Moore, a grown white man running for the Senate, who is a pedophile.

Because the image is primal, we have a White Sky Daddy working with his beloved White Son-of-Sky Daddy to build a better world for people who look like he does. Their fingers may eventually touch. So be afraid. Be very afraid.

2. CBN News, "'We Want God.'"

Because we are indeed *symbol-using, symbol-making, symbol misusing animal(s), inventor of the negative, separated from [our] natural condition by instruments of [our] own making, goaded by the spirit of hierarchy, and rotten with perfection,* we are at a moment of great peril. Just as Christian nationalism is rising, we must confront the fact that the God most Christians worship is the image of the party leader.

2

A War of Aggression

The Moody Formation of
American White Christian Nationalism

ALAN JAY RICHARD

In 1884, the American Federation of Labor called for direct action starting May 1, 1886, if a federal eight-hour workday was not enforced by that date. Chicago labor organizers enthusiastically participated in this effort. Chicago's Cyrus McCormick, managing partner of International Harvester and founder of the McCormick reaper plant, was notorious for using technology to simplify work, and then lowering wages and forcing skilled workers to either work more hours for less pay or be replaced by new workers.[1] In 1885, he pushed further cost-cutting measures despite record profits. When workers went on strike, other business leaders pressured him to back down, fearing a general strike. Instead, he fired top labor organizers. On May Day the following year, thirty-five thousand Chicago workers walked off their jobs. Tens of thousands marched peacefully that day and the next. But on May 3, police at the McCormick reaper plant fired at striking workers and killed two. A protest meeting was planned for May 4. Only a few thousand showed up, however, and the invited speakers failed to appear. The meeting was almost over with less than two hundred still in attendance

---

1. Green, *Death in the Haymarket*, 105.

8

when the first dynamite bomb ever used in peacetime in the United States was hurled. Police panicked, and in the darkness shot some of their own as well as strikers. In the end, seven police and four workers were killed in what became known as the Haymarket Affair.

This incident launched the Moody Bible Institute and a host of associated institutions that would transform not only evangelicalism but American Christianity in a lasting way that is still not fully understood. By 1885, Dwight Lyman Moody, already regarded as the greatest evangelist of his generation, had become convinced that revivals like his required lay "Christian workers" to do preliminary and follow-up work if they were to reach the new immigrants who were swelling the ranks of Chicago's working class. Moody had already founded separate Bible colleges for girls and boys in his hometown at Northfield, and he regarded these as models for the kind of training he wanted to offer.[2] He had been trying for months to persuade McCormick and other members of his network of business allies to fund a training school for equipping "city lay missionaries" to do urban door-to-door evangelizing and visitation for and between revivals.[3] Since Moody had evangelized working-class Chicagoans in the 1850s and 1860s through his Sunday school and YMCA revitalization, he thought he knew how this could be done. As of 1886, his pleas for support had gone unheeded. In a fundraising appeal in the October 1885 issue of his publication *Record of Christian Work*, "Dynamite or Gospel," Moody warned readers that reaching the masses was not an abstract goal, since "some of the unreached are restless and have organized for aggressive work of their own."[4] He reminded them that "the Socialists had a parade of 5,000 strong in Chicago," and that speakers of this parade bragged that "Chicago has 20,000 Socialists of whom 8,000, it was said, were armed." The rise of the socialist menace "is a loud call to the better class to carry the gospel without delay to these people." A single riot "would destroy more property in a day, at the hands of such an organized force, than it will cost to carry the gospel to every soul in Chicago, and to erect and endow a training school for Christian workers." The "introduction of these restless elements," he concluded, makes it important to begin this work without delay. In a January 1886 meeting during which he promised to unveil more details about his proposal, he once against stressed that "what should be done for the

2. Findlay, *Dwight L. Moody*, 313.

3. Gloedge, *Guaranteed Pure*, 54.

4. Moody, "Dynamite or Gospel," 2

workingmen" is "the greatest subject before the people of today," and insisted that reaching the wage earners in factories and shops, "the bone and sinew of society," was vital because of their vulnerability to the appeals of labor and socialism.[5] Paternalistic approaches, he said, create the impression "that we look upon them as a sort of poor beggars that cannot help themselves," untrained Christian workers are unable to counter their skeptical arguments, and ministers talk above their heads. The solution was to recruit and train "workers from out of the ranks" and train them because "they know these poor people—how they live and what they need." Again, Moody insisted on urgency: "Christianity has been on the defensive long enough," he said. "The time has come for a war of aggression." Instead of funding the institute, business allies funded another Moody revival, scheduling it to coincide with the planned May strike. But Moody's repeated warnings after Haymarket resulted in a mayoral ban on public meetings, prematurely ending the revival; the McCormick family coughed up one hundred thousand dollars, and other members of Chicago's business elite supplied the remaining one hundred fifty thousand.[6]

The institutions, technologies, and personalities that subsequently surrounded Moody's Institute formed a bridge between the religious reconsolidation of a unified white American nationalism, following what Mark Noll has called the "theological crisis" of the Civil War and the ideological and technological reshaping of Christian nationalism into a reliable tool of neoliberalism. The early republic's Christian nationalism had been the provenance of the northeast—first in New England and then in New York—and it rested on the notion that a disciplined community (an empire of New England towns and small farms) and universal literacy together entailed the proper vehicle for salvation.[7] The ecumenical missionary societies (the American Tract Society, the American Bible Society, and the American Home Missionary Society) were the institutional expressions of this Christian nationalism. This Christian nationalism was paternalistic, chartered, and corporate; it was capital-intensive, was built around print campaigns, and aimed to foster a coherent, unified sense of religious and political meaning. So it eschewed theology in favor of ethics and maxims. The societies were organized like banking institutions—the Bank of the United States served as model for the American Bible Society—and their

5. Gloedge, *Guaranteed Pure*, 57.

6 Ibid., 59.

7. Haselby, *Origins of American Religious Nationalism*, 193.

officers belonged to the political and economic elite, not the intellectual or clerical elite.[8] But this form of Christian nationalism was a minority faith, and it was in tension with the revivalist religion of the frontier that it aimed to civilize. This frontier religion was largely indifferent to national identity. It was hostile to what it regarded as the improper support that governments provided to the mission societies and their apparent attempt to control the means of the production of salvation. And revivalist religion was suspicious of theological gatekeepers who got between the Bible and the individual believer, including seminary-educated clergy.[9] In the 1830s, Jacksonian rhetoric created a fragile but workable appropriation of both the paternalistic and imperialistic aspects of northeastern Christian nationalism and the frontier revivalist suspicion of capitalism, centralized bureaucracy, and erudite elites.[10] Jacksonianism gave the Methodists, Baptists, and other revivalists in the Ohio River Valley a stake in nation building; and the president's attacks on both the missions to the Indians (replaced by his removal policy) and the Bank of the United States echoed the frontier resentment toward the Christian nationalism fueling the missionary and Bible societies. Jacksonianism also aligned frontier homesteaders with the planter class for the first time. As a perusal of Jackson's 1830 State of the Union address confirms, it did all this by replacing civic republicanism with whiteness as the unifying feature of national identity. It was national and it was evangelical.

But in the next two decades, this fragile unity would be broken. With it, the evangelical consensus that frontier revivalism had created, and which was already marginalizing the Protestantism of the northeast, would split violently in two. The frontier-evangelical resistance to erudite, academically trained mediators rested on a conviction that the Bible not only was divinely inspired but spoke so plainly that anyone who could read the words on the page could also, with the help of prayer, discern their meaning once the distractions of tradition were removed.[11] This belief drew on the Reformation's *sola scriptura* rhetoric, on the popularization of Scottish commonsense philosophy, and on the romanticized figure of the unlearned but wise and self-reliant backwoodsman. B. M. Pietsch has called this belief "republican perspicuity," which was "not grounded in the authority of

8. Ibid., 242, 245.

9. FitzGerald, *Evangelicals*, 27–28.

10. Haselby, *Origins of American Religious Nationalism*, 315.

11. Noll, *Civil War as Theological Crisis*, 19.

the masses or shared experience, nor in any particular method, but on the sovereign right of each individual to interpret as he (or, more rarely in the nineteenth century, she) saw fit."[12] Pietsch's parenthetic qualification, of course, is important especially considering subsequent history. This "republican perspicuity" was not equally distributed. It was universal, in the sense that it was male and white.

On one level, republican perspicuity presented itself as a fundamentally democratic notion. Indeed, Jeffrey Robbins has argued that, in severing the link between state and church authorities and the interpretation of God's will, this American democratic faith was the instantiation of the death of God.[13] But as Mark Noll points out, republican perspicuity yielded no plain, simple, transparent, and shared meaning of Scripture in the debate over slavery.[14] For white evangelicals on both sides of the debate, the very existence of passages in the Bible indicating approval or tolerance for slavery seemed to force a choice: either abandon the principle of republican perspicuity, substantially relax the principle of scriptural authority (William Lloyd Garrison), or acknowledge God's approval of slavery in the abstract if not in the concrete form of cotton plantation chattel slavery (Princeton Theological Seminary's Charles Hodge). The principle of republican perspicuity doomed nuanced, contextualized arguments because these were seen, either to add something outside of Scripture to Scripture, or to deny the ability of common folk to properly understand Scripture without the assistance of elites. Noll asks why this crisis did not extend to African American evangelicals or to evangelicals abroad who shared with white Americans both the principle of perspicuity and a high view of Scripture, or why it didn't lead any major defender of slavery to suggest that slavery be extended to whites.[15] Of course, as Noll also suggests, the answer lies in the interdependence between the powerful construct of whiteness for sorting and re-sorting populations, the usefulness of the rhetoric of whiteness for securing both land and free labor for the large-scale cotton farming that built the nation's economy, and the sense American national identity. These mutually validating cognitive, affective, and economic structures meant that "most of America's white Bible believing Christians" on both sides of the slavery debate viewed racial issues "with commonsense solutions derived

12. Pietsch, *Dispensational Modernism*, 97.
13. Robbins, *Radical Democracy and Political Theology*.
14. Noll, *Civil War as Theological Crisis*, 31–50.
15. Ibid., 54.

nether from the Bible nor from the historical storehouse of Christian moral reflection," and these solutions largely determined what seemed plain in the Bible and what didn't.[16] The earlier Jacksonian synthesis of paternalism and individual independence, of imperialism and distrust of centralized authority, left American Christian identity and American Christian destiny resting on nothing but the "common sense" of a shared whiteness through which tensions internal to religion in America could be resolved. Post-Jacksonian Americans could regard "foreign" attempts to judge their national policy in the same way frontier revivalists regarded northeastern missionaries, and the "common sense" of shared whiteness meant that with few exceptions, African Americans were regarded as the topic of debate and not as interlocutors.

The resolution of the institution of slavery through force of arms rather than through the clear light of Scripture threw republican perspicuity into serious question. The professionalization of biblical scholarship and its separation from ministerial training, symbolized in the 1880 founding of the Society of Biblical Literature (SBL), was one attempt to address this question, resting on the assumption that the meaning of the text could be found in the historical conditions of its production. As Hector Avalos has observed, the SBL was also part of a postwar "culture of professionalism" serving "to validate an emerging middle class."[17] The reliance on historical-critical methods not only entailed an abandonment of the principle of republican perspicuity (while individual devotional Bible reading was good and fine, it could not yield the authoritative meaning of the text) but professionalized a field of inquiry and created a gap between the language of scholars on the one hand and the language of both pastor and flock on the other.[18] This gap played into the hands of post-Reconstruction Confederate ideology, its influence more powerful than ever after the capitulation of northern politicians and even religious abolitionists such as Henry Ward Beecher and Harriet Beecher Stowe to demands of southerners to end efforts at justice for African Americans.[19] White southerners wanted reconciliation with white northerners, but on their own terms: no equality for African Americans, no attempts to prevent cotton planters from coercing labor so long as it wasn't technically slavery, and no admission that

16. Ibid., 52.

17. Avalos, "Ideology of the Society of Biblical Literature."

18. Pietsch, *Dispensational Modernism*, 58–59.

19. Blum, *Reforging the White Republic*, 13.

republican perspicuity was in any way compromised. Northern white industrialists, Moody's primary financial supporters, wanted a gospel that encouraged a disciplined workforce and discouraged labor unrest. From the inception of his revivals in the 1870s, Moody's preaching answered these desires. Moody emphasized the ethical duty of forgiveness and reconciliation between northern and southern whites, and increasingly opposed social reforms that purported to be enacted in the name of the gospel. Moody himself staged segregated revivals in the south,[20] a practice that earned him the opprobrium of African American church leaders, one of whom said, "I would not have him preach in a barroom, let alone a church."[21]

Moody's Chicago Bible Institute, later the Moody Institute, also rescued the principle of republican perspicuity by pioneering an alternative professionalization of scriptural interpretation that read the biblical text as an encyclopedia for answering practical questions and sought the meaning of the text not in the conditions of production but in the internal relationship of parts to whole, down to the determination of the meaning of individual words. Moody's Institute also created or promoted resources to support these practices, including concordances, study guides, and the Scofield Reference Bible. Although the Institute sought and obtained the prestige associated with academic achievement and formal theological training (its first director, R. A. Torrey, having been trained at Yale), its methods were drawn more from the technical tools of business management, law, and accounting than from those of critical history, philosophy, or theology.[22] The aim was not to discover what was at stake for the biblical writers at the time of a text's production, but to discover what the text as the revelation of eternal truth tells *me* about *my* practical life and work, here and now. These methods were distilled not only in the form of courses (eventually correspondence courses) but also in books and periodicals, the most important being topical guides to biblical passages, chock-full of graphs, charts, and taxonomies.

They were accompanied by other spiritual technologies (e.g., prayer ledgers) designed to relieve uncertainty regarding God's will. In the hands of the Institute, the "second baptism" experience promulgated by the Holiness movement was transformed into a simple technology. Moody had gone to England to preach revivals at the invitation of Keswick Holiness

20. Ibid., 120–45.
21. Findlay, *Dwight L. Moody*, 288.
22. Gloedge, *Guaranteed Pure*, 104.

clergyman William Pennefather, and had become comfortable with the Keswick movement after it repudiated its teachings about moral perfection and spoke instead of the Holy Spirit's power.[23] In his *Secret Power* (1881), Moody also borrows the Keswick Holiness movement's shift in the context of the Spirit's power from home to work.[24] With the preface, Moody's book announces that is not a theological tract but a practical guide to accessing "this power from on high" without which "our work will be drudgery." For Moody, the Holy Spirit is "the secret of efficiency" and the power of success.[25] R. A. Torrey later fleshed out Moody's procedure for obtaining this power. In *The Person and Work of the Holy Spirit* he explains the seven steps for receiving the baptism of the Holy Spirit (acceptance of Jesus as personal savior, renunciation of sin, open confession, absolute surrender, intense desire, precise "definite" prayer, and belief that it has been given), justifying and specifying each step with multiple decontextualized verses from the Scriptures.[26] The last step is crucial because, as Torrey explains "true assurance comes through the Word of God," and since these seven steps are the Word of God's guarantee of baptism by the Holy Spirit, the believer believes that the event has occurred once the believer completes the procedure.[27] These technologies, being "Biblical," would be unfailingly effective, so that Moody could say that he could not see "how a man can follow Christ and not be successful."[28]

The Institute's most pervasive single influence on contemporary Christian nationalism was perhaps the promotion of the Scofield Reference Bible, which balanced the prestige of scholarly imprimatur with the reaffirmation of republican perspicuity: anyone, with proper diligence and the proper tools, could become a Bible expert without specialized formal education.[29] Like other products associated with the Institute, the Scofield Reference Bible was built around methods borrowed from law, business, and engineering. Scofield, a former attorney, framed the Bible's copious notes around the question of what in the Bible was and was not directly obligatory to contemporary humanity. Scofield's reliance on engineering

23. Findlay, *Dwight L. Moody*, 116.

24. Gloedge, *Guaranteed Pure*, 67.

25. Moody, "Dynamite or Gospel," 1–2; Moody, *Secret Power*.

26. See Torrey, *Person and Work of the Holy Spirit*, 129–86, especially 175.

27. Moody, *Secret Power*, 237.

28. Gloedge, *Guaranteed Pure*, 44.

29. Mangum and Sweetnam, *Scofield Bible*, 171.

methods leads him to declare the charting of time into periods "marked off by distinct limits" to "have the same relation to right understanding of the Scriptures that correct outline work has to map making."[30] The Scofield Reference Bible's influence reached further than fundamentalism because it became regarded as the best resource of its kind for American Christians who rejected higher criticism on the grounds of white republican perspicuity. It became the unofficial Bible of Pentecostal denominations, in spite of its attack on the exercise of the gifts of the Holy Spirit central to Pentecostal practice.[31] It became the Bible that missionaries took with them. And it became ubiquitous among mainline denomination members as well, in spite of repeated denominational attempts to discourage this.[32]

The political and social ideology of Moodyism was not just explicitly announced in the aids to study and personal development that the Institute distributed; the ideology was embedded in the methods used to transmit them. Both salvation and the baptism of the Holy Spirit, for instance, became wholly individualistic; the baptism of the Holy Spirit was achieved simply by claiming the promises of the Bible for equipping Christian workers—just as a prospective employee entering into an employment contract would give the employer authority (a metaphor Torrey frequently used). Community was virtual and consisted of individuals within and apart from various denominations who had established a "personal relationship" with Christ and who diligently took upon themselves the tasks of Bible study, prayer, and evangelism. Denominationalism and even church affiliation became entirely secondary. A proper "dividing" of God's Word would reveal clearly that the old postmillennialist notion of a social and moral preparation for Christ's return was wrong, that the preaching of Christ himself in the Sermon on the Mount and elsewhere does not apply to our time, and that, indeed, attempts to use levers of power improve life materially illegitimately protects working people from exposure to events that might lead them to submit to the will of God and give their lives to Christ. Moody's dispensationalist reasoning insisted that social reform was "repainting the pesthouse," and that beyond a certain point it was literally godlessness.[33] Reality itself is structured like a business; God, the beneficent employer, legally obligates himself to automatically respond to procedures outlined

30. Scofield, *Addresses on Prophecy*, 13.

31. Mangum and Sweetnam, *Scofield Bible*, 174–75.

32. Pietsch, *Dispensational Modernism*, 211.

33. Gloedge, *Guaranteed Pure*, 15.

in his Word. Moody's complex of correspondence courses, revival and training structures, annotated Bibles, practical tracts, and (later) radio and television media developed independently of traditional ecclesiological or academic authority and so fostered a distinctly American white therapeutic Christianity whose new "common sense" was derived from the professions that circulate around corporations: engineering, law, and management.

Moody's influence extended beyond fundamentalism and Pentecostalism. The most influential Christian nationalist figures of the mid-twentieth century, Spiritual Mobilization's James Fifield Jr. and Norman Vincent Peale, were raised by fathers who were followers of Moody's Institute. Fifield's father and namesake, a Kansas City Congregationalist minister, was an enthusiastic Institute associate, contributing to the *Record of Christian Work* and speaking at the Institute's conferences.[34] Fifield himself has been described as theologically "liberal" pastor, but the mode of biblical reasoning in his writings, his "practical" engineering approach to spiritual methods as tools for success, and the close association he makes between godlessness and worker's movements all exhibit habits of thought and feeling grounded in Moodyism.[35] Peale's father, a physician turned Methodist pastor, was also a "Moody Christian" with an attachment to the practical procedures, the emphasis on self-reliance, the revival technologies, and the fierce opposition to labor reform he associated with it.[36] Through the Spiritual Mobilization organization, Fifield and Peale's anti-New Deal activism opposed "pagan statism" to "freedom under God," and set the template for the Eisenhower era's use of domestic religious propaganda as a weapon in the Cold War.[37] For Peale and Fifield, "freedom under God" meant the free market, and anything that challenged it was "pagan statism." Importantly, Peale and Fifield also combined the "freedom under God" message with biblically referenced individual practical self-help manuals—Fifield in his early megachurch work and Peale in his books, lectures, and *Guideposts* magazine.[38] The therapeutic anticommunist Christianity of the 1950s was Moodyism without biblical inerrancy.

This combination of practical individual self-help with jingoistic patriotism and stridently libertarian economic views inseparable from

34. Fifield, "Development of the Local Church," 817–18.
35. Kruse, *One Nation under God*, 9–11.
36. George, *God's Salesman*, 20–21.
37. Kruse, *One Nation under God*, p. 92.
38. George, *God's Salesman*, 103–24.

religion itself, aimed directly at religious consumers and cutting across ecclesial and academic gatekeepers, was pioneered by Moody and his associates and bursting the confines of American evangelicalism during the age of quiet desperation that was the 1950s. Thus, Moody should not be regarded primarily as an influence on American fundamentalism. White American Christian nationalism today is in part an outgrowth of Moodyism. It is rooted in a reaffirmation of a "white Christian republic" after the crisis of the Civil War. It is motivated to forget and forgive systemic injustices when these are perpetrated by white Bible-believing Christians. It has little respect for genuine theological dispute, creeds, or denominational boundaries. It promulgates an approach to the Bible and indeed to Christian existence grounded in law, engineering, and business that preserves the principle of republican perspicuity in spirit, an approach that yields alternative facts. It shapes a sense of self and world through methodology, so that the "truths" it proclaims seem to result from individual discovery, from "thinking for oneself." And it opposes the "freedom under God" of the individual understood as an enterprise in a market with recourse to divinely certified self-help procedures to the "pagan statism" of any movement, religious or political, that would compromise that freedom by interfering in the market on the side of working people. Although it is far from the only factor contributing to the Christian nationalism that reared its head in the fall of 2016, Moodyism's influence on Christian nationalism is profound and worth of a closer look. It is an often-subterranean, persistent, and multidimensional war of aggression on behalf of a reconstituted white neoliberal republic fought with the weapons of corporate power, with business, legal, and engineering methods, and with the perennial appeal to republican perspicuity.

3

This Is How We Talk Here, and If You Don't Like It, Leave

Theological Epistemology, Information Technology, and Christian Nationalism

S A R A H   M O R I C E   B R U B A K E R

Under what conditions is it appropriate—or necessary, or even unavoidable—to set rules for how people are permitted to talk in one's community? What should the consequences be for transgressions? How, if at all, should rule violators be banished? Who gets to decide when a rule has been violated, and who gets to issue consequences?

This question may be, and indeed frequently has been, sounded in a Christian theological register. What were the early christological controversies and the ecumenical councils if not the hashing out of sanctioned theological speech and its mode of enforcement? But this set of questions sounds in other registers too, and in new ways, enabled and reframed by technological developments. In this essay, I shall suggest that rules for theological discourse in the English-speaking theological academy, and rules for discourse in English-speaking online social media communities, share some important similarities. While they do not share a common trajectory, at moments their respective trajectories peak, veer, double back, and dip in tandem. I shall suggest, further, that each trajectory is affected by economic, political, and intellectual developments that go back to the 1970s at least, and that such understanding is crucial for confronting the alarming rise of Christian nationalism.

From Blogger.com to Charlottesville

An optimistic and countercultural spirit characterized the early days of social media, according to José van Dijck in her 2013 book *The Culture of Connectivity: A Critical History of Social Media.* "Between 2000 and 2005," van Dijck writes, social media platforms "thrived on the enthusiasm of users as they ran and operated their new virtual spaces, which were often regarded as experiments in online citizenship and a reinvention of the rules for democratic governance."[1] Anyone with an internet connection could claim a space in which to convene a conversation, and then lay down rules for what constituted acceptable discourse in that space. "If you don't like it here, you're free to leave"—a sentiment one could imagine coming from the mouth of an antiunion employer toward workers—was used against people who attacked online communities' ground rules. And why not? Without clear rules and a mechanism to mute violators, any conversation about (for example) feminism would quickly be drowned out by a thousand comments consisting of variations on the theme, "Get back in the kitchen and make me a sandwich." Moreover, if someone disliked the rules in one community, they could simply move to another or start their own for free. The internet was not about to run out of personal blogs, personal websites, Facebook pages, Twitter accounts, or YouTube channels.

I was a pseudonymous blogger at a prominent feminist blog in the mid-2000s, which coincided with my doctoral studies in theology. It is hard to overstate the optimism of those blogosphere days. Thanks largely to our ability to block, ban, or otherwise cast out those who wished to sabotage our community, we could at long last hold extended conversations without interruption. Communities of marginalized people formed, unhindered by geography. Writers from minoritized communities, who would have stood little chance at getting past the gatekeepers of traditional media, amassed huge online followings. Their words began to matter in national political discussions. They were getting literary agents and book contracts and speaking engagements. These communities were changing how people thought, spoke, and strategized.

1. Dijck, *Culture of Connectivity*, 15.

Writing from the far side of 2016, I am inclined to look upon our optimism with wistful kindness. Some contemporary commenters, though, take a more critical approach. Following the rise of the alt-right, the 2016 presidential election, and the deadly Unite the Right rally in Charlottesville, some have asked, did the online American left unknowingly encourage the ascendancy of the alt-right?

Angela Nagle, in her book *Kill All Normies: Online Culture Wars from 4Chan and Tumblr to Trump and the Alt-Right*,[2] certainly thinks so. Nagle notes that the "libertinism, individualism, bourgeois bohemianism, postmodernism, irony, and ultimately the nihilism that the left was once accused of" now characterizes the meme-driven online alt-right subculture. Although that subculture is reckoned as conservative, it "more Fight Club than family values, more in line with Marquis de Sade than Edmund Burke." To be sure, Nagle does not suggest that these formal similarities themselves bestow blame upon the left. Following the analysis done by Simon Reynolds and Joy Press in *The Sex Revolts*,[3] Nagle suggests that the alt-right is within a lineage that values, as an end in itself, transgression against the dominant culture. In the 1950s, such transgression might target white Christian America. But in the 2000s, being transgressive meant rebelling against what Nagle calls "Tumblr liberalism," a target of particular scorn for Nagle.

Young, educated, and media savvy, Tumblr liberals—or SJWs,[4] in the more common parlance of their critics—are characterized, according to Nagle, by an extreme constructivist understanding of identity, particularly gender identity. They also, she suggests, exhibit a fondness for targeted public shaming. In the 2000s and early 2010s, these sensibilities exercised tremendous influence upon the shape of online discourse. In fact, even before the rise of the alt-right, some on the left criticized these characteristics of online progressive activism. The late Mark Fisher, in his 2013 essay "Exiting

2. Nagle, *Kill All Normies*, 2017.

3. Reynolds and Press, *Sex Revolts*, 1996.

4. SJW is an abbreviation for "social justice warrior," and it became a term of opprobrium during the Gamergate controversy of 2014, a targeted campaign of online criticism and harassment against video game developers Zoë Quinn and Brianna Wu, and feminist media critic and blogger Anita Sarkeesian. The incident that touched off the controversy was the publication a long blog post by Quinn's ex-boyfriend, accusing her of unethically seeking positive media attention from a journalist with whom she was in a relationship. It quickly coalesced into a movement composed mostly of young men reacting negatively to feminist criticisms of sexist video game tropes, and by extension to feminism in general.

the Vampire Castle," called left-wing Twitter "a miserable, dispiriting zone," its spokespeople "horrifyingly high-handed" and "dupe-servants of the ruling class; and Fisher opined that "it pays lip service to 'solidarity' and 'collectivity', while always acting as if the individualist categories imposed by power really hold."[5] Any unity exhibited by its members, suggested Fisher, is rooted not in solidarity but "mutual fear—the fear that they will be the next one to be outed, exposed, condemned." These criticisms resulted in Fisher himself being publicly shamed, a fact noted at the end of Nagle's book when she discusses the callous and crowing responses from SJWs to the news of Mark Fisher's death by suicide.

The nascent alt-right saw a political opportunity in the missteps of Tumblr liberalism and social justice warriorhood. Casting SJWs as the dominant culture against which they were transgressing, and having been banned from progressive online spaces, purveyors of antileftist vitriol started their own communities and campaigns characterized by "aestheticized revolt." Possibly this provided some consolation in the face of their existential and economic vulnerabilities. While the alt-right counts the occasional woman and Boomer among its ranks, Nagle points out that the majority of its footsoldiers are young white men a generation or more removed from assumptions of lifelong monogamy, home ownership, and job security. It is here that Nagle exposes the contradiction at the heart of alt-right[6] existence. As much as its rhetoric expresses longing for a patriarchal white culture unsullied by consumerism, capitalism, feminism, multiculturalism, and individualism, the actual activity of alt-right foot soldiers bears little resemblance to this vision. The online troll living in his mother's basement may be a stereotype. But in fact the data suggest that young, white, unskilled white men without four-year degrees often live with relatives, delay marriage, and spend many hours a week playing video games and watching porn.

In what sense, if any, is the alt-right Christian? It is a slippery question since so much alt-right discourse consists of meme sharing and

5. Fisher, "Exiting the Vampire Castle."

6. The contested distinction between "alt-right" and "alt-light," while tremendously significant to some adherents, is beyond the scope of this paper. Briefly, the alt-light putatively emphasizes civic nationalism rather than the ethnonationalism and white racial identity rhetoric of the alt-right. However, the Anti-Defamation League notes that the alt-light operates in the orbit of the alt-right; and that while the former may reject overt displays of white supremacy, it nevertheless "embraces misogyny, anti-Muslim bigotry and xenophobia." Anti-Defamation League, "ADL Resource."

"shitposting," the practice of sharing aggressively bad content on websites and discussion forums. If one is looking for a systematic theology of the alt-right, one will be disappointed. (Indeed, some on the alt-right mock religion by brandishing tokens of allegiance to the pseudoreligion "Kekism" or "Cult of Kek," in which the object of worship is Pepe the Frog.) Prominent alt-right figure Richard Spencer, a key organizer and speaker of the Charlottesville Unite the Right rally, is less circumspect about his religious views. Christianity, Spencer tells the *Atlantic*'s Graeme Wood, makes false claims; indeed, he himself is an atheist. Yet he also expresses longing for something "as robust and binding as Christianity had once been in the West." According to Wood, Spencer understands his mission to include fostering "a consciousness of [white people's] identity as whites with a shared Christian heritage."[7]

This coalescence of nationalism, identitarian organizing, reactionary politics, cultural nostalgia, economic and existential malaise, theological opportunism bordering on nihilism, and emerging technology: none of it is unprecedented. We need only go back to the 1970s to see an earlier concatenation of many of the same factors.

Version 1.0

The information landscape the United States currently inhabits took shape, according to sociologist Manuel Castells, in the 1970s. It was during this decade that the name Silicon Valley was coined and then stuck; the first microprocessor and microcomputer were invented; and the first commercially successful microcomputer, the Apple II, was introduced. Amid spasmodic cultural change fueled by the Vietnam conflict and the antiwar movement, by *Roe v. Wade* and Watergate, this technological change "did not come out of any pre-established necessity; it was technologically induced rather than socially determined."[8] Even so, technological developments did help to shape the response to cultural upheaval. For one thing, the emergence of information technology bequeathed to U.S. industry generally certain "milieux of innovation," in Castell's words. Discoveries would need to be tested in "research centers, higher-education institutions, advanced-technology companies, a network of ancillary suppliers of goods and services, and

7. Wood, "His Kampf."
8. Castells, *The Rise of the Network Society*, 60.

business networks of venture capital to finance startups."[9] These milieux, once consolidated, would draw on expertise and investment from around the world.

This combination of consolidation and globalization fit well with wider economic restructuring. Along with the cultural spasms of the 1970s came economic ones, in the form of oil and global monetary crises and rampant inflation. Employers saved money by relocating to low-cost areas and laying off employees, availing themselves of the latest technological innovations to pick up the slack. Cities around the globe moved from goods-oriented to service-oriented economies, portending an eventual missing middle in the wage structure. Meanwhile, nations ended the Bretton-Woods monetary system in favor of floating currencies, leading to less insular national economies; this, in turn, facilitated the proliferation of multi- and transnational corporations.

Perhaps it is no surprise then that nostalgia for a simpler time caught hold of the popular imagination. In 1971, as historian Michael Kammen recalls, *Time* magazine published a piece titled "The Meaning of Nostalgia" because nostalgia suddenly seemed to be everywhere. Two years later, in 1973—the year of the *Roe v. Wade* decision, a major oil crisis, and the withdrawal of American troops from Vietnam—*Newsweek* ran a story on historical tourism, which had by then become big business. Consumers, weary of social turmoil and looking for a heritage, flocked to theme parks where they could experience colonial days or the life of a frontier family. "Americans," the article said, "seem to want to see and touch anything old— the genuine old, if possible, but even the hokey and plastic 'old' will do if nothing better is available."[10]

Nostalgia, as Kammen points out, is "likely to increase or become prominent in times of transition, in periods of cultural anxiety, or when a society feels a strong sense of discontinuity with its past."[11] Such was the case in the 1970s. In addition to the economic upheaval mentioned earlier, the 1960s had left traditionalists worried about various liberation movements while "the newly liberated themselves would not (or could not) rely upon conventional roles, relationships, and assumptions to steer them through stages of the life course."[12] Nostalgia, though, does not simply involve a

9. Ibid., 65.

10. Kammen, *Mystic Chords*, loc. 12905.

11. Ibid., loc. 12905.

12. Ibid., loc 12918.

longing to return to the past as it was. As Svetlana Boym explains, even the word nostalgia gives away the contradiction: the word itself is only "nostalgically Greek," a seventeenth-century portmanteau of two Greek roots: νόστος, *nóstos* ("return home") and ἄλγος, *álgos* ("longing"). It was coined by Swiss doctor Johannes Hofer in 1688, while thinkers like Gottfried Leibniz and Isaac Newton were busy working out modern astronomy and mathematics. Hofer defined *nostalgia* as "the sad mood originating from a desire to return to one's native land." By coining the term, Hofer simply put a word to what other physicians were noticing among recently displaced people. At the time, this longing was taken as a medical problem, for which opium, leeches, or a trip to the Swiss Alps might provide some relief.[13]

Americans in the 1970s skipped the leeches but did seek to identify and maintain a heritage for themselves through local historical preservation efforts, through the aforementioned living history museums, through commissions, genealogical research, back-to-the-land experiments, and civic groups devoted to appreciating local or national history. So pronounced was this fixation that Kammen calls it "heritage syndrome," and in fact the Heritage Foundation was itself an expression of heritage syndrome when it was founded in 1973. Kammen rightly warns of the ambiguity of heritage. Reverence for heritage "can lead, and has led, to commercialization, vulgarization, oversimplification, and tendentiously capricious memories." But Kammen, a historian, also sees potential in heritage. It can, he notes, be a "powerful stimulus to the popularization, and hence to the democratization, of history."[14]

The 1970s were not the 2010s, and the religious right—whose seeds were sown in the 1970s—are not the alt-right. Nevertheless, I believe progressives in 2018 would do well to look for lessons in the Christian theological nostalgias of an earlier decade. For the 1970s yielded a strain of theological nostalgia still influential today, albeit in mutated versions displaying varying degrees of comfort with Christian nationalism.

In January 1975, a conference was held at the Hartford Seminary Foundation. Out of that conference came the Hartford Declaration, a jeremiad against modernity and mainline Protestantism. The idea for the conference, according to evangelical theologian Richard Mouw, came from Richard John Neuhaus and Peter Berger. Neuhaus, formerly a leader in Clergy and Laity Concerned about Vietnam, was beginning his rightward shift

---

13. Boym, "Future of Nostalgia," 217.
14. Kammen, *Mystic Chords*, loc 13128.

and would eventually become a founding editor of the conservative journal *First Things*. Berger, a sociologist, was a "politically homeless conservative," in the words of Gary Dorrien, "who [found] his way to the neocon Right."[15] Neuhaus and Berger, on Mouw's account, thought it would be fun to make a list of the aspects of mainline Protestantism that annoyed them.[16] The list turned into a gathering, and out of the gathering came a statement, later published in *Worldview* magazine, excoriating what the authors took to be mainline Protestant notions. Sentiments singled out for condemnation by the signers included such as, "Modern thought is superior to all past forms of understanding reality"; "Religious language refers to human experience and nothing else, God being humanity's noblest creation"; "All religions are equally valid"; and "The sole purpose of worship is to promote individual self-realization and human community."[17]

Those familiar with liberal Protestantism may recognize these claims as still holding sway in many mainline settings. To put those claims in some context, Randall Balmer warns—helpfully, I think—that the post–World War II ecumenical movement elided theological distinctiveness in the name of Christian unity, in the process "align[ing] itself, more-or-less uncritically, with white middle-class American culture."[18] The Hartford Declaration, accordingly, rails against mainline Protestantism's inability to distinguish its own convictions from those of the dominant culture. But perhaps most noteworthy about the Hartford Declaration is its list of signatories, and the theological perspectives some signers would go on to espouse. Those who signed the statement included Mouw, Neuhaus, and Berger, but also George Lindbeck and Stanley Hauerwas (among many others, including William Sloan Coffin, a liberal theologian who would later repudiate the statement).

This is a curious and tantalizing tidbit, at least for our present purposes. Lindbeck and Hauerwas, though they differ theologically in some respects, are both associated with the postliberal theological school. Postliberal theology holds that Christians are a people constituted by distinctive narratives, linguistic conventions, and communal practices. Therefore Christians need not justify their claims according to the standards of other rival communities and their discourses—of which modernity is one. To

---

15. Dorrien, *Social Ethics in the Making*, 489.
16. Mouw, "Hartford: A Reminiscence."
17. "Appeal for Theological Understanding."
18. Balmer, *Thy Kingdom Come*, loc. 709.

be fair, Hauerwas and his students and supporters typically reject American Christian nationalism as a corruption of the Christian gospel. But it is worth noting that sentiment with which I have titled this essay—"This is how we talk here, and if you don't like it, then leave"—applies just as well to postliberal theological habit as it does to progressive social media communities.

Then, too, there is this interesting data point: the Hartford Declaration emphasized that Christian proclamation need not be, and indeed *must* not be, acclimated to the dominant culture. Even today in North American academic theological circles this is generally held to be an epistemologically defensible position, arguably more respectable than straight-up biblical inerrancy. (More than once I have heard people describe postliberalism as an academically respectable theological home for those disillusioned by the evangelicalism or fundamentalism with which they were raised.) Yet the Chicago Statement on Biblical Inerrancy, which also emerged out of 1970s reactive nostalgia, came out three years *after* the Hartford Declaration, which raises the question of how exactly the influence runs. Held side by side, the two statements portend some of the fault lines that would organize the American religious right following Jerry Falwell and the Moral Majority's ascendancy in the 1980s. The Hartford Declaration would point the way for postliberal academic theologians and the most intellectual of the theoconservative think tank set. The Chicago Statement, meanwhile, was backed by such figures as Francis Schaeffer, J. I. Packer, R. C. Sproul, and Hal Lindsey, all of whom would enjoy long-standing prominence in what is more popularly thought of as the religious right. I wonder if, rather than using each trajectory as a foil for the other, one might understand *both* theological trajectories as being influenced by 1970s nostalgia, which was itself born of economic and cultural upheaval and technological future shock.

All of this, of course, leads one to consider similarities between the 1970s and today. Again, the alt-right is not the religious right of a generation ago, nor is the alt-right kin to postliberal theology. But if we consider the lessons of the 1970s, we might wonder whether a certain combination of factors—a shrinking middle class, growing income inequality, increasing globalization, progressive cultural victories, and rapid technological innovation—make for an environment in which nostalgic, identitarian theologies are likely to take hold and (thanks to the new technology) spread. If that possibility proves compelling, then perhaps we progressives might consider the implications of banishing dissident voices from within our midst. As I think back to my time in the progressive blogosphere, I wonder whether it was prudent to banish everyone we banished. On the other hand, what choice did we have? The onslaught of harassment meant that we either banned people from commenting at the first whisper of trouble or quit blogging. At the same time, I know something now that I did not now then: To justify our heavy-handedness, we invited people to start their own antifeminist online communities if they didn't like how we ran things. I realize now that they did exactly that.

4

Donald Trump and the Privilege of Outrage

JAMES HOWARD HILL JR.

"I wish you could know
What it means to be me . . ."
—NINA SIMONE

"Should we cry when the Pope die? My request:
We should cry if they cried when we buried Malcolm X."
—TUPAC AMARU SHAKUR

To possess outrage is to possess privilege. This, of course, is not a privilege that should engender shame; summoning the spirit of outrage is nothing less than a testament to the fact that, somewhere within the dampened bowels of your conscience, something shook you. For many, shock is the spirit that hovers over the teeming waters that will one day become outrage. For others, shock performs an annunciation of sorts, preparing the body for a rupturous event soon to come. Shock can also operate on a cosmic, seemingly universal level alerting people the world over that the shock they feel must decrease so that the greater, transformational work accomplished through outrage may increase. Consequently, very few should be surprised that throughout the U.S. and abroad millions of people have become outraged by the actions and attitudes of the forty-fifth president of the United States of America, Donald J. Trump. They are outraged because his acts have categorically shocked them, and out of the chaos of said shock, disgrace and shame were produced. However, while millions of U.S. citizens were bequeathed with a newfound resistance born out of Trump's Ares-like ascendancy to power, *outrage* is not a term I care to use when describing my posture towards the current administration. Allow me to explain.

As a Black scholar whose interior life has been mercilessly scourged by terroristic acts of white epistemic violence committed both inside and outside the academy, I relinquished all rights and privileges to certain forms of politicized outrage a long time ago. Truth be told, many communities of color have recited apoplectic dirges from the catacombs of our racialized being long before Trump began publicly calling African and Latinx countries shitholes. This is the paradox of the Black scholar; the nature of our work requires us to perpetually produce Black thought for the same people and institutions that simultaneously defile, demean, and devalue the requiems we compose in commemoration of Black life deemed disposable by the state. Black feminist and womanist scholars have easily produced the most groundbreaking theoretical interventions in the fields of critical race theory, law, politics, and theology over the last forty years, yet remain perpetually disrespected by tenure committees who always seem to discover novel ways to deny the new wine they *claim* their old wineskins so desperately require; this accounts for why, all around us, the academy seems to be bursting through its seams.

Why do Black scholars continue to produce intellectual labor for spaces that convulse at the mere sight of our embodied interventions? Why do we aspire to teach knowing that departments unabashedly place fetters around our minds and yokes around our necks; fetters and yokes they, themselves, were never created to carry? Why did I agree to undertake this project and provide thoughts about a racist president who, at his worst, is only a feeble, etiolated avatar of my *true* enemies? There remains, however, a host of reasons why, despite every legitimate reason to leave this vocation, Black scholars continue set our face like a flint towards tomorrow and continue the work. Though many of our reasons are sacred, communal, and consequently unspeakable here, three aspects of our work, despite our best attempts at abandonment, bind us to the call. Those three aspects are the Black scholar's roles as exorcist, healer, and herald of a futurity unseen.

The Black Scholar as Exorcist

To be a Black scholar is to be an exorcist, whether you desire to put on the collar or not. For Black scholars, creative work is always already conjuring work. Before committing our hands to a project, we already know that our research contains methodologies we could never include in institutional proposals or abstracts. Besides articles, monographs, and archives, our work requires us to access the cloud of martyrs (or witnesses) that exists not merely beyond us, but rather through us, beside us, and within us, as Christina Sharpe's concept of "wake work[1]" poignantly demonstrates. This means consulting the words of Ida B. Wells-Barnett as well as remembering how the touch of our grandmother's calloused hands and the prescient glow of her knowing eyes unlocked worlds of wonderment and possibility the likes of which C. S. Lewis could never fathom.

I am always fascinated when white scholars come up to me and ask, "How does it feel to be a Black scholar in the age of Trump?" How does it feel? How does it *feel*? In that moment of inquiry, what metric are you looking for me to provide you? How did it feel to be a Black scholar writing in the necropolitical afterlife of Hurricane Katrina? How did it feel to be a Black scholar writing under Nancy Reagan's "Just Say No" campaign? How did Ida B. Wells-Barnett *feel* as an organic intellectual and activist under the reign of William McKinley? I could use the remainder of this chapter to outline innumerable violent, necropolitical white women and men who, though they used every political technology available, were not able to suffocate Black folks' capacity to collectively write, organize, teach, revolt, dance, and love in the iridescent glow of defiance. If history has revealed anything it is that the task of the Black scholar who writes in the region of the shadow of death includes possessing the belief that our imagination can provide the down payment for the substance of things hoped for as well as the earnest of a world unseen.

Black scholars are equipped with the burden and privilege of using our gifts as intellectuals and creatives in the service of unmasking the spirit of cishetero-patriarchical-white supremacy and calling it by its true name. One of the principal responsibilities of the Black scholar writing within a Trumpian dystopia is to make abundantly clear that while we must contest with the flesh-and-blood reality of Trump's hamartiological will to destruction, spirits and principalities exist in high necropolitical places, which

---

1. For future reading, see Sharpe, *In the Wake*.

suture, sustain, and necessitate the power codified in Trump's fetid flesh. This is what many white scholars fail to realize. To truly destroy the principalities that provided the conditions that led to a Trump presidency is nothing less than to inaugurate the destruction of entire worlds that benefit them. Though many leftist scholars may find Trump's presidency abhorrent, how many of them have ever materially combatted the white origins of their own faculties, disciplinary fields, and promotions? If their idea of liberationist commitments does not include demanding the destruction of the countless Trumps who hold positions of power in their sphere of influence, they can keep their hot takes and performative militancy. Are we really going to sit here and pretend like Trump's presidential cabinet does not look like most liberal faculty directories?

The Black Scholar as Healer

To be clear, healing is not synonymous with reconciliation. Black scholars are not called to be life coaches whose intellectual production exists solely to make white folks feel better about themselves, their power, and their world. When I speak of Black scholarship performing a healing work in troubled times, I am primarily speaking of how Black scholars engage, as Saidiya Hartman once put it, "the mortuary of the archive"[2] in order to consecrate the dignity of Black life and make known the quotidian nature of Black death. Though many scholars have rallied around the Trump administration's mobilization of the term *fake news* to quell the rising tide of dissent, the history of Black people in the United States could be analyzed as the discourse of a people whose mere enfleshment signifies the racialized biomythography of the United States; this signification constitutes, perhaps, the greatest piece of fake news ever constructed in colonial modernity. The United States believes that if there is a celestial body of divinities, they exist solely to bless the global, Protestantized aims of U.S. empire and condemn any form of hostile resistance; Black scholars are surrounded by a cloud of Black martyrs, known and unknown, who sonorously shake the cosmos in seraphic refutation.

Black scholars are exorcists, and the exorcism of white epistemic claims on Black life and Black death is nothing less than a healing, holy, and elect work. What does it mean to commit to the work of healing during this Trumpian dystopia? The sad reality is that many, if not most, of the

---

2. For further reading see Hartman, *Lose Your Mother*.

answers lie in the work of the Black women we simply refuse to invite to panels, welcome as conference speakers, or name as department leaders. The solution exists in nothing less than acknowledging that many so-called allies are completely fine with the fact that the panels, conferences, and departments in question are *their* property—fine with the reality that the role of the Black scholars, particularly Black women, is only rendered legible in proximity to white power and white control. Quite possibly, the work we accomplish as Black scholars will amount to little more than codifying the vicissitudes of our reality for future generations lest the truths of our experiences become locked away within us in a poisonous ossuary concealing our right to be angry.

The Black Scholar as a Herald of Futurity

Black futurity cannot be easily assimilated into the eschatological demands of Christian colonial modernity because it doesn't necessitate a progressive, teleological end. Black futurity is not a liberal utopia. To possess a praxis of Black futurity does not mean longing for a future where white folks learn to become benevolent rulers; Black futurity imagines a world of renewed and continued existence where the colonial epistemologies and governmentalities of the Western world are reduced to theatrical phantasmagoria for the amusement of those who overcame by the word of our testimony and the blood of both lambs and panthers. While, at first glance, Black futurity may seem to be little more than an exercise in innocuous, theoretical fabularity, it is important to remember that Malcolm X was anathematized from the U.S. political imaginary because his conceptualization of a Black future did not match the political eschatology of Western liberal modernity. Nina Simone was primed to be a pop superstar until she was pneumatologically besieged by cloven tongues of conviction that inspired her to compose such imprecatory psalms as "Mississippi Goddam" and the apocalyptic dirge "22nd century." Find me a Black person who dared to publicly envision a future where white folks were not the chief educators, scientists, artists, and lawmakers, and I will show you a Black person who faced countless necropolitical technologies constructed to choke them with the troubles of this world such that many of them never reached the full width, breath, and maturity their brilliance earned and demanded.

To be a Black scholar in the age of Trumpian dystopia requires the same thing that has been required of Black scholars since our visceral inception; we must dare to view our research as rosebushes planted in the region of the shadow death. Like the rosebush, our work is planted in defiance and blooms in opposition. Contrary to popular belief, things do grow and beautify in darkness. The work of Black scholars proves to the world that light can be overrated.

Today Donald J. Trump is president. Three years from today, I may wake up in a world where Donald Trump is still in power. Though I will fight with every fiber in my being to oppose the avatar in chief, I am far more invested in tending to my rosebush.

Do my roses shock you?

5

The White Christian Nationalist Hustle

Since the election of Donald Trump, a great many political commentators, scholars and activists have asked about the meaning of the terms *nationalism* and *patriotism*, and *populism* and *democracy*. Are they interchangeable? Are they equivalent, either morally or politically speaking? If not interchangeable or equivalent, then what differences and distinctions can we draw? What lessons can we learn about the ways the former have been allowed to define—and as I will argue, cheapen and degrade—the latter? And how is it that race—more specifically, the American legacy of white supremacy and racial inequality—factors into the equation? It will be my argument that the end result of the conflation of nationalism with patriotism and populism with democracy is the political project of white nationalism, not only from which the presidency of Donald Trump draws support but also to which Trump and his presidency provide succor. Even more, while the white nationalists might have given Trumpism a bad name, the nationalist populism, like the cultural politics of the Religious Right a generation prior, is in fact a ruse to provide cover for an internationalist, corporate agenda.[1]

In his "Notes on Nationalism," first published in war-torn England in 1945, George Orwell provides us with what is still a helpful distinction between nationalism and patriotism. He writes with emphasis that "*Nationalism is not to be confused with patriotism.*" He insists that the two terms

---

1. I have been persuaded of this latter point by Klein, *No Is Not Enough.*

are not only distinct, but opposed to each other. Whereas nationalism "is inseparable from the desire for power," patriotism "is of its nature defensive, both militarily and culturally."[2] Nationalists believe in the rightness of their cause, no matter its actions or effects. Nationalism operates on a moral plane beyond good and evil and thus by definition subscribes to the myth of its own exceptionalism. Patriotism, by contrast, while sharing with nationalism a sense of devotion to a particular place, culture, set of public institutions, and way of life, does not absolve its nation from critical moral scrutiny. It rejects the "love it or leave it" mentality and instead affirms the need to make the nation's union "ever more perfect." In this way, patriotism is not nostalgic for a lost past; its project is not restorative, but transformational, remaining open to what the future may become. Put otherwise, the nationalist is essentialist; the patriot anti-essentialist. The nationalist believes the nation's identity either was, or can be, fixed, its people clearly defined, its borders impenetrable, its constitution static and unchanging, whereas the patriot, to borrow the formulation from Julia Kristeva, sees the nation and its people, culture, and institutions as always "in process/ on trial."[3]

What of the relation and distinctions between populism and democracy? Like the pairing of nationalism and patriotism, it would be a mistake to read populism and democracy as synonymous. According to Cas Mudde and Cristobal Rovira Kaltwasser, coauthors of *Populism: A Very Short Introduction*, *populism* has no meaning on its own. Or better, it operates only as a "thin-centered ideology," and therefore must attach itself to more fully fleshed out ideologies either from the left or right of the political spectrum.[4] So there can be both left-wing populism and right-wing populism; it can be either revolutionary or conservative. Even so, it has certain character traits—most notably, in spite of its claim to represent more faithfully the genuine will of the people, it tends to be divisive, driven by an "us vs. them" mentality that is as moralistic as it is antagonistic. In Mudde and Kaltwasser's words, populists split society into "two homogenous and antagonistic groups: the pure people on the one end and the corrupt elite on the other."[5]

---

2. Orwell, "Notes on Nationalism." The entire essay is worth reading, especially for Orwell's identification of the dangerous character traits of nationalism, which still seem very much in evidence today within the American political landscape.

3. See Kristeva, *Revolution in Poetic Language*.

4. Mudde and Kaltwasser, *Populism*, 6.

5. Ibid.; quoted in Friedman, "What Is a Populist?"

By their moral valuation of purity and corruption, they are able to claim the right that they alone represent the people. In this way, populism is seen to function as a political cleansing. Because there is such confidence in the rightness of the cause, there tends to be a certain willingness to forgo or sacrifice the public institutions, deliberative process, civil dialogue and decorum, and even the basic rule of law that characterize democratic culture and governance. The history of populism tells a tragic irony—namely, populism becomes the very thing it despises, exclusionary and corrupt. In the words of Jan-Werner Müller, "What the establishment supposedly has always done, populists will also end up doing. Only with a clear justification and, perhaps, even a clear conscience."[6]

Enter Trump, or better, the America First campaign envisioned by Steve Bannon and other alt-right forces plotting for years against the elite establishment. As the journalist Joshua Green has chronicled in his book *Devil's Bargain*, Bannon's ambition and agenda have always been larger than being a mere political advisor to Trump. As Green has put it, "[Bannon] is the narrative thread that runs through not just the rise of Trump, but the rise of the whole right-wing populist, nationalist politics that he has been espousing."[7] His aim has been nothing less than a wholesale cultural revolution that is hard-right and nationalist, to be sure, but also global in its aspiration. Bannon's genius, Green suggests, was not merely to traffic in and propagate conspiracy theories—though this was certainly not beneath him or the Breitbart News website he oversaw—but to employ a team of researchers who would provide the evidence that understaffed media outlets, who no longer had the resources to invest in investigative journalism, would accept wholesale as a giftbox ready to run as a scoop all their own. In this way, Bannon managed to take the alt-right from the fringes to the mainstream. New media were marshaled to disrupt, to obfuscate, to confuse, and to short-circuit the system with such an overflow of facts and "alternative facts," of news and "fake news," that the very prospects of truth and transparency can be dismissed as quaint. In this "post-truth" moment, reality has become a fungible asset.

The particular populist, nationalist politics of the Trump–Bannon alliance first came to expression in terms of strong borders and the hard line on immigration. The case was made that this was not about race, but about what would be good for those who have been left behind in the changing

6. Ibid.

7. Goodman, "Joshua Green on the Devil's Bargain."

labor force of the global economy. America's magnanimity must be more strategically employed, more targeted, held in reserve in this time of austerity and crisis. Border control, so it has been claimed, is not about keeping Mexicans or Muslims out, but about providing—or at least reserving—jobs for "real" Americans. As Trump has made plain, most especially in his address to the United Nations General Assembly, making America "great again" is not about restoring our leadership or moral authority in the world, but about asserting our sovereignty in a world of supposed disappearing boundaries and borders, a world of global economic trade and partnerships, of transnational corporations, and so forth.

Interestingly enough, it was Hitler's crown jurist, Carl Schmitt, who made the concept of sovereignty the centerpiece of his political theology, who argued that in the technocratic world of liberal democracies the state had lost the capacity to decide. The restoration of sovereignty was the solution to the problem of political legitimacy in the age of mass politics. And so, he opens his defining work from 1922 *Political Theology* with the line, "The sovereign is he who decides on the exception."[8] This state of exception has been seized upon time and again in supposed democratic governments around the world as a way of suspending the civil liberties and the constitutional order more generally. All in the name of saving it.

Another interesting connection here is the work of the American constitutional law scholar from Yale, Paul Kahn, who has written extensively on the (non)relation between political sovereignty and the rule of law. As Kahn sees it, the rule of law operates by reason whereas political sovereignty is an expression of the will. The triumph of the rule of law leaves no space for the sovereign decision. It is as if once the rule of law has been firmly established, our government could operate on autopilot, a self-regulating system run by technocratic functionaries (i.e., the elite establishment). While it promises regulation, order, and fairness for all, it fails to fully appreciate what makes a nation, a society, or a people. Just as the Frankfurt school taught us how the modern Enlightenment age of reason was integral to, or eventuated in, the justifications for colonial imperialist subjugation and a century of nearly total war, so too does Kahn argue that a political philosophy under the spell of reason alone is insufficient for understanding how human society actually works. Reason fails to account for the will, just as the rule of law disavows the revolutionary violence upon which it rests. Archetypal stories are told and retold of the role of political revolution in

8. Schmitt, *Political Theology*, 5.

the founding of the state—that is to say, of revolutionary war as the suspension of the established order of law—of the sacrifices necessary for the maintenance of the state, and of the monopoly on violence that is integral to the state's promise of law and order. This is not a justification of political violence or an argument for revolution, but instead a diagnosis of the fuller picture necessary for an adequate conception of the political. Whereas a political theology that attends to the concept of sovereignty helps us to recognize the violence of origins and the originary violence upon which the modern liberal order rests, the (re)assertion of sovereignty is a fundamentally political act that wittingly or unwittingly invokes the specter of violence to upend or disrupt that carefully constructed order.

In this way the assertion of sovereignty is integral to populism—both negatively in terms of its grievance, and positively in terms of its concept of the political. In addition, also in this way nationalism so easily provides the ideology that populism lacks. Specifically, nationalism provides the necessary figuration of the people upon whom the claim of legitimacy for the exercise of popular sovereignty rests. It is not that a singular and settled identity is the only means by which a national identity can be constructed and understood, but this is precisely the point. Adopting the rhetoric of national identity as if it is known and under threat but nevertheless can be remembered and ought to be restored is a way of thinking identity in stark contrast to the multicultural, the multinational, and the miscegenated. This populism fueled by grievance not only is co-opted by white nationalists but also is the very mechanism of white nationalists, who invoke and revel in a romanticized memory of the nation's great past without considering the nation's past sins.

While some have argued that the modern democratic practice of popular sovereignty eventuates in a diffusion and dispersal of power with almost anarchical implications,[9] critics note that the assertion of sovereignty operative within today's populist politics is more unified and traditional. The democracy of populist nationalism no longer operates as the political instantiation of the death of God; on the contrary, it is more like the triumphant return of religious orthodoxy wherein the structure of power remains wholly intact. In the words of Saul Newman, "It sees itself as a wresting sovereignty back from the control of elites who have sacrificed it on the altar of globalism, who have watered it down and reduced it to technocratic

9. See Robbins, *Radical Democracy and Political Theology*.

governance."[10] When wed to nationalism, the politics of populism requires a strong nation predicated on a singular notion of a unified people. Though not necessarily racist or even racialized, insofar as the power, privileges and prerogatives of white America have (been perceived to have) lost their stranglehold on the culture and institutions of American public life, this serves up the cipher of grievance by which the fictive construction of the national identity might be projected.

So to return to Trump—or more precisely, to Trumpism in terms of his America First nationalism originally plotted by Bannon—the emphasis on sovereignty is not of minor importance, and the undertone of violence is not coincidental. The argument is made that after over half a century policing the world, propping up international organizations, rebuilding war-torn nations, and selling out our manufacturers to the promises of free trade, it is time to reset our sights at home. But, of course, this is not the full truth. The hard line on immigration also entails demonizing immigrants, not only as those who would take jobs from hardworking Americans, but even more as rapists, drug lords, criminals, and killers.[11] Combine this with Trump's Islamophobia, misogyny, birtherism, and condescension toward African Americans—condescension sold as outreach (to wit: "What the hell do you have to lose?"). In addition, remember the president's condescension (if not hostility) toward Puerto Ricans—condescension sold as relief in the wake of Hurricane Maria (to wit: Trump's running arguments with San Juan mayor Carmen Yulin Cruz over delays in U.S. federal response to the hurricane; and the spectacle of Trump's eventual Puerto Rican visit during which, in a show of magnanimity, he tossed rolls of paper towels to a roomful of U.S. citizens depending on government assistance). Add to this Trump's initial refusals to disavow former KKK grand wizard David Duke while campaigning, and his equivocations in responses to Charlottesville. Consider too the president's advice to NFL owners in the wake of player protests initiated by Colin Kapernick: Trump called protestors sons of bitches and told team owners to insist that their athletes (most of whom are African Americans) "shut up and play." Before that, of course, Trump had picked a fight with a gold-star military family who had lost their son in Afghanistan, and had insinuated that because the family was Muslim the father of the slain service member was silencing his grieving wife.

---

10. Newman, *Political Theology* (forthcoming).
11. See Moreno, "9 Outrageous Things."

Why in the face of these mounting offenses do I still read on my Facebook feed from avowed evangelical Christians (and family members) posts such the following: "I'm thankful that we have a President who will say words like these, including 'Scripture', 'the Lord', 'God', and 'praying for you' [all with no 'PC' qualifiers], while many politicians—and his opponent last November—are already pouncing on the 'opportunity' the Las Vegas tragedy provided to jump on political bandwagons"? Why, as we learned from exit polls, did 80 percent of white evangelical voters support Trump when he so brazenly violates their moral norms, shares so little with their cultural heritage, and appears so biblically and theologically illiterate?

The better question is, how do we separate the man from the movement? Is Trump merely the empty vessel in Bannon's larger movement? Is Trump—either the brand or the carnival barker—a necessary ingredient to make the once unsavory palatable? To turn a takeaway point from J. D. Vance's *Hillbilly Elegy* into a question, is it really true that appearing to be a racist has no negative consequences in relation to the president's appeal and success? (Vance's book became a best seller and explained Trump's success to those who had not seen it coming.) If Trump's racism has not put a damper on his political success, then why did the U.S. Senate candidate from his party, Roy Moore (a sexual predator), receive 80 percent of Alabama's white evangelical vote whereas 95 percent of black evangelicals voted against Moore? The religion scholar Charles Mathewes has written elegantly of the damage being done to the Christian faith in America by what he diagnoses as white Christian fear of, and opposition to, pluralism. In an opinion piece in the *Washington Post* titled "White Christianity Is in Big Trouble. And It's Its Own Biggest Threat," he writes, "When we've reached a place where good Christian folk think it's a matter of major theological principle not to sell pastries to gay people but are willing to give pedophiles a pass, I think it's safe to say that American Christianity today—white American Christianity in particular—is in a pretty sorry state."[12] We were told in 1924 by W. E. B. Du Bois that "the problem of the twentieth century will be the problem of the color line."[13] Likewise, Martin Luther King Jr. held up a mirror to American religiosity when he told us the "appalling" truth that what we already knew—"that the most segregated hour

12. Mathewes, "White Christianity."
13. Du Bois, *Souls of Black Folk*, 15.

of Christian America is eleven o'clock on Sunday morning."[14] We might say that the more things change, the more they stay the same.

Consider also Thomas Frank's *What's the Matter with Kansas*: the argument there is that the elevation of cultural politics—which is largely credited to the successful political mobilization of the evangelical right—has blinded people to the consequences of their support for a conservative economic agenda. What is left untold is why and how the evangelical Right was politically mobilized in the first place. The case of Jerry Falwell is instructive here, both in how it exposes the hypocrisies at work and anticipates the vampire-like effect of the evangelical right's current iteration. In 1965 Falwell famously delivered a sermon titled "Ministers and Marchers," in which he argued "that our only purpose on this earth is to know Christ and to make him known." He continued by saying, "Believing the Bible as I do, I would find it impossible to stop preaching the pure saving gospel of Jesus Christ, and begin doing anything else—including fighting Communism, or participating in civil-rights reforms."[15] This sermon expressed the traditional evangelical stance toward the proper relationship between religion and politics—namely, that there is none. The sole purpose of the Christian faith was the saving of souls. This theological vision aligned perfectly with the long-standing support of the evangelical community for the strict separation of church and state. By Falwell's reckoning in 1965, this was the gospel in its purest form.

What must be noted, of course, is that this sermon comes only two years after Martin Luther King Jr.'s "Letter from a Birmingham Jail," a statement defending the coordinated campaign of marches and sit-ins, which King penned in direct response to "A Call for Unity," a statement made by eight white Alabama clergymen rejecting his methods. And so, Falwell's defense of ministers, against the marchers, must not be misconstrued as some generic statement or theological treatise on the purity of the gospel; rather it must be seen as the racialized code that it was—a theological defense of white Christianity. This is the monstrosity that lies within: an evangelical identity distinctly southern and white. Self-identifying evangelicals entered into the fray of the civil rights movement only to denounce it in the name of spiritual purity.

This truth becomes even more evident when in 1980, one year after Falwell cofounded the Moral Majority, a conservative lobbying group that

---

14. King, *Papers of Martin Luther King, Jr.*, 6:149.

15. Quoted in DeMar, "Old and New Jerry Falwell."

at its height claimed more than four million members and two million do-nors, he urged in his book *Listen, America!* that it was the Christians' duty to rally together to fight for family values, the free enterprise system, and patriotism. Borrowing from the playbook of the African American church's leadership in the civil rights movement, Falwell and others adopted a full-scale politics of grievance, claiming simultaneously to be composed of a majority of God-fearing Americans and to be persecuted by a hostile secu-lar culture led by liberal elites and activist judges. It was a generational shift and a wholesale theological revolution. The political mobilization of the evangelical Right would become a pillar in the Republican Party's southern strategy and would cement the support of so-called Reagan Democrats for decades to come.

Just as Steve Bannon's work has recently brought white nationalism from the fringes to the mainstream, so decades earlier Falwell's success was that he helped bring born-again, evangelical Christianity from the fringes to center stage. And nowhere was this evident that in the person of George W. Bush. It has been well chronicled that Bush's candidacy was a calculated political strategy built on the realization that a national candidate able to shore up the evangelical vote was assured of electoral success. Bush was the first and only mainstream presidential candidate whose credentials as a member of the evangelical Right were unquestioned. But by the end of Bush's second term, not only had he endured plummeting public support, but the faith-based agenda he had sought to promote had been discredited and left for dead. Enter Bannon and Trump, to feast on the remains, the distillation, of white Christian grievance minus any soul-saving promise or ambition. Monstrosity in its purest form is what is left over after the religious pretense is gone: a moral majority in the form of vigilante justice, a white Christian nationalism emboldened to make America great again.

I have titled this chapter "The White Christian Nationalist Hustle." I call white Christian nationalism a hustle for still another reason altogether: We have seen the dangers of calling nationalism patriotism, of calling populism democracy. We have also seen the dangers of constructing and mobilizing evangelical identity politically as distinctly southern and white. What is most horrifying and revealing simultaneously is how once defen-sible terms, *patriotism* and *populism*, have been given a bad name. It was once said that Hitler gave racism a bad name. This was not meant to suggest that before Hitler racism was any less insidious, degrading, dehumanizing, and deplorable. But the scientific or cultural arguments for the supremacy of the Aryan race that once had been broadly defended and supported could no longer be made in good conscience after they had been embraced and employed to such destructive effects in the Holocaust. The point here is not that the German population, who served as Hitler's "willing executioners," should have known better. Rather, exposed moral rot is only perceived when the complicity is complete.

We stand poised at a like moment of reckoning. Populism has been stripped of its democratic credentials. White evangelicalism has forfeited its soul. And the real hustle that we have not yet even begun to realize is how even nationalism is a ruse. Just as the cultural politics of the right has led to an entire generation to vote against their economic interests, so the grievances of white nationalists have been mobilized to provide cover for what is essentially an internationalist, corporatist agenda. While Trump might speak of restoring America's greatness by reasserting its sovereignty, his willing accomplices put up with the chaos and disgrace in service to their corporate paymasters.

Over the past couple years, we have seen a slew of moral condemnations and political pleas that have taken the form of "a special place in hell is reserved for . . ." The first condemnation came from former secretary of state Madeleine Albright while she was campaigning for Hillary Clinton, and in comments for which she later expressed public regret, who said that there was "a special place in Hell for women who don't help each other."[16] And after Ivanka Trump would say that there is the special place in hell "reserved for people who prey on children," in reference to allegations of sexual predation against Roy Moore, Bannon would offer a rebuttal of sorts when he said that the special place was reserved for "Republicans who should know better," in order to make the case for the importance of electing Moore to the U.S. Senate in spite of voters' possible misgivings.

For my druthers, I prefer the more stirring vision of hell provided to us by Dante wherein hell is what we make of it. Or more precisely, the hell we live is the hell of our making wherein our own particular sin is magnified for all of eternity. If it is true as the history plainly shows that the evangelical right was politically mobilized by a sense of white grievance, and if it is true, as Mathewes and others are presently arguing, that white Christianity in America has substituted fear for love as its organizing center, then the hell we have birthed has been very long in the making. And with or without Trump, or before or after, there is no redemption in sight.

16. See Albright, "My Undiplomatic Moment."

6

Ungrounded Innocence

Confronting Christian Culpability in White Nationalism

KAREN BRAY

Let me begin bluntly: we cannot confront the problem of Christian nationalism if we claim that it is not *real* Christianity. In examining the role Protestant Christianity played in the second rise of the Ku Klux Klan, Kelly J. Baker suggests,

> The desire to set up the boundaries between true and false religion does nothing to further the scholarly enterprise . . . presenting the religion of the Klan as false religion allows an assumption that religion is somehow not associated with movements and people who might be unsavory, disreputable, or dangerous.[1]

Baker continues, "the order launched campaigns to unify Protestants across denominational lines in its efforts to save America from immigration and other 'evils.' The Klan was a part of the religious story of the nation, whether its members were likable or not."[2] When we indulge the desire to distance ourselves from those we find disreputable, we refuse to engage the full scope and weight of the religious story of America. Too often, those of us who are Christian, those of us who work within post-Christian and Christian theological traditions, and those of us who teach at Christian-affiliated colleges and seminaries hesitate to identify ourselves with such unsavory roots. By

1. Baker, *Gospel according to the Klan*, 17–18.
2. Ibid., 19.

45

underidentifying the ways in which the disciplines and faiths we inhabit are infused with this legacy, we eclipse our responsibility to dismantle the systems that grew from the toxic soil. In the proclamation of our relative innocence, we risk cheap redemption, when deep reckoning is what's due.

The interconnection between white supremacy and Christian nationalism, can of course be traced further back to the very establishment of the United States as both a sovereign nation and an economic power. In *Stand Your Ground: Black Bodies and the Justice of God*, womanist theologian Kelly Brown Douglas explores the genesis of what she calls our "Stand Your Ground" culture. Stand your ground culture marks whiteness, and white Protestant Christianity, as sovereign property. As Douglas notes, "for [the Puritans], building an Anglo-Saxon nation . . . meant building a Protestant Christian nation."[3] Such religious legitimation marks white supremacy as divinely ordained. It ties Christianity to the construction of "whiteness as cherished property."[4] When such property is trespassed on, white Christianity has God's permission to "stand its ground." As Douglas starkly puts it, "a myth that declares the 'supra-status' of a group of people compels a sense of destiny that is bound to turn deadly."[5] In a stand your ground culture, George Zimmerman can kill Trayvon Martin with impunity, while we all know that if Martin had shot Zimmerman the same would not be true. Having no rights to even self-possession, self-sovereignty means that under stand your ground culture there is no property black people are supposed to count as theirs; there is no ground on which to stand.

According to Douglas, the development of this culture can be traced to American "founding fathers" enamored with the myth of Anglo-Saxon purity held over from Tacitus's *Germania*, the AD 98 treatise that marked ancient Germans as an exceptional race.[6] The same founders' fears of the mixing of the blood of European colonists and African slaves amplified the ability of non-Anglo-Saxon European immigrants to become white, while non-Europeans could not.[7] The transcendence of European immigrant identity into whiteness and so into Americanness was fortified through the religiosity with which the Puritans and Pilgrims imbued the myth of the

3. Douglas, *Stand Your Ground*, 10.

4. Ibid., 41–42.

5. Ibid., 14.

6. Ibid., 5.

7. Ibid., 36.

nation. This mythicohistory becomes a liturgy, ritually repeated as justification for who could count as properly American.

Our civil religion and Protestant Christianity are handmaids to, or perhaps the architects of, a white supremacist and nationalist culture. There is no easy way out of the structures the two have built. White Americans, and in particular white Christian Americans (Christian by practice or by heritage), cannot distance ourselves from this history; it is our collective inheritance. It is the liturgical stuff in which we have been forged. Hence, we must better attend to the ways our own attempts at distance have left us culpable. As a political theologian deeply engaged with affect theory, I want to approach this problem through an affective register. Three affect-laden orientations (at least) continue to defer the accounting of what is owed: those of obedience, innocence, and persecution.

We cannot understand the phenomenon of Donald Trump if we do not attend to the affect of obedience—or more precisely of submission to an authority's plan. If the inheritance of whiteness as cherished property is Godly sanctioned, then an affective draw toward an authoritarian figure parsing out punishments for those who question white sovereignty seems inevitable. In an essay written in the wake of the 2016 election, historian of religion Kathryn Lofton encourages us to look to the recent study by political scientist Matthew MacWilliams. MacWilliams, "reported findings that a penchant for authoritarianism—not income, education, gender, age or [even] race—predicted Trump support . . . The results suggest that the voter wants somone whose authority makes others around him submit to his will."[8] Such a desire for submission is familiar to any scholar of American religion or practitioner of contemporary Christian evangelicalism. Charismatic pastors wield authority, and the congregation obeys. This liturgical training combined with Americanism as Christian predestination nurture a desire for clarity over to whom to submit and whom to count as the real Americans, the truly elect.

The draw toward submission to an authority's plan is amplified by an affective pull towards innocence and the repulsion from guilt. An affective drive towards innocence is the terrain I am treading in my work at Wesleyan College in Macon, Georgia. Recently our community has begun to acknowledge our twentieth-century ties to the Ku Klux Klan and the symbols, rituals, and institutional sensibilities that have persisted. For instance, so-called sisterhood traditions included the class name, the "Tri-K Pirates,"

8. Lofton, "Understanding Is Dangerous."

and rituals of initiation that involved upperclassmen donning hooded robes and leading first-year students around by nooses. These traditions continued well after the first African American women entered the college in the 1960s. It was not until the 1990s that some of the Klan iconography and the nooses and hoods were retired.[9] Even within a student body that is today around 30 percent black and over 20 percent international many sisterhood symbols and rituals (albeit sans nooses) persist. The history of these traditions, and the abhorrent iconography and images that accompanied them, have mainly lived "peacefully" in our archives for 180 years. Each time this history surfaced, those raising the issue were met with moods of denial, including accusations that they were "spreading false information." Claims to religious and gender innocence were proffered: Methodist *women* could not have done this. While some on campus are finally open to reckoning with this history, others, including alumnae, current students, faculty, and staff still do not acknowledge the scope of the problem or how denialism and minimization allow white supremacist legacies to continue. The cries of, "It wasn't me!" have been legion.

In an interview given to Bill Moyers on the then upcoming book *The Cross and the Lynching Tree*, James Cone warns us that if America cannot get over its "innocence," we will never be able to build the beloved community.[10] Obstacles to claiming our guilt are fortified by our stand your ground culture. Douglas suggests that "[white space] travels with white people. It is the space that white people occupy. This space is not to be intruded upon, hence the right of whiteness to exclude."[11] If it is my God-given right to exclude, then I need not feel guilt or shame. I am innocent. At Wesleyan, White Christianity inhabits innocence. Such a sense of innocence is represented in the covert and overt Christian supremacy that imbues the atmosphere of the campus. Christianity pulses in rhetoric around faith and servant leadership, in the invocations that open faculty meetings, and in the deployment of "good Methodism" to claim racism could not have been at the heart of our sisterhood traditions. Such reasoning goes something like this: these rituals could not be racist, because Wesleyan women have been followers of Jesus. To claim otherwise is to shake what is owned by Wesleyan sisters (at least its white sisters), the cherished property of womanly civility *and*

9. For coverage of Wesleyan's racial history see Schrade, "Macon's Women's"; and Schrade, "Ga. College."

10. Moyers, Interview with James Cone.

11. Douglas, *Stand Your Ground*, 42.

Christ's blessing. The need for both collective and individual pardon, the fear of shame and guilt, risks killing Wesleyan's soul; it has been killing our country, and quite literally many of our countrypeople.

To confront our discomfort with the mood of guilt, we must also acknowledge additional moods, those of possessiveness and persecution. For many white people and white Christians in particular, it seems as though proclamations of innocence are not sufficient; one must also proclaim the guilt of those pointing out the fallacy of such innocence. Whiteness and Christianity are innocent; those that trespass on their grounds are guilty. This dynamic is at play whenever someone calls Black Lives Matter a hate group, or when right-wing pundits pontificate about "the war on Christmas." It is at play in the rallying call, "Jews will not replace us." It pulsates behind:"Make America Great Again," because it affirms that "America" is under attack by the very idea that nonwhite and non-Protestants might have their own ground in this country on which to stand. This persecution complex is the inevitable affective combination of the divinely ordained right to kill those who would challenge our standing, *and* the much more subtle affective attachment to innocence over guilt. The former is easier to identify because it manifests itself quite literally in a body count. The latter takes more careful attention because it involves a more expansive reckoning: it involves realizing where we too have wanted to have our debts forgiven, and so where we too have had blood on our hands.

So what is to be done? Are there alternative affective registers with which we might become more finely attuned?

Perhaps there is some hope in the reclamation of a more complex divine economy. In the past I have been drawn to theological critiques of atonement. I find the argument proffered by womanist theologian Delores Williams—that atonement theology encourages those already marked for surrogacy and suffering, namely black women, to remain in such a position—utterly convincing.[12] As a member of the indebted generation, I prefer to define worth apart from economic accounting. And yet, in facing an incessant drive toward "American innocence" embraced by Christian nationalists, we must revisit such theologies and rethink what parts of atonement and of debt paying we might reclaim.

Such an accounting would necessarily subvert the accounting that sticks bad debts on African Americans. According to Stefano Harney and Fred Moten, so-called bad debt is used to mark the unpropertied, to mark

12. Williams, *Sisters in the Wilderness*.

blackness as precisely that which does not have proper standing. Harney and Moten encourage those already marked as unprofitable to remain fugitive from sovereignty so as to resist the very modes of relation that marked them as a bad investment in the first place.[13] But this need not mean that those of us marked as good investments should ignore to whom our profitability is indebted. We must reconcile with just how bad our credit is. To do so would be to sit with our sin. It might be to refigure atonement figurations: to move away from a clean account that can be paid and forgotten, and to move toward a figuration of attunement, of greater attention—indeed of greater attention to all for whom we are never supposed to stand.

Perhaps this is what is requested in the recent *New York Times* op-ed by feminist essayist Roxanne Gay. In her response to President Trump's infamous "shithole countries" comment Gay writes:

> I am tired of comfortable lies. I have lost patience with the shock supposedly well-meaning people express every time Mr. Trump says or does something terrible but well in character. I don't have any hope to offer. I am not going to turn this into a teaching moment to justify the existence of millions of Haitian or African or El Salvadoran people because of the gleeful, unchecked racism of a world leader. I am not going to make people feel better about the gilded idea of America that becomes more and more compromised and impoverished with each passing day of the Trump presidency.
>
> This is a painful, uncomfortable moment. Instead of trying to get past this moment, we should sit with it, wrap ourselves in the sorrow, distress and humiliation of it. We need to sit with the discomfort of the president of the United States referring to several countries as "shitholes" during a meeting, a meeting that continued after his comments. No one is coming to save us. Before we can figure out how to save ourselves from this travesty, we need to sit with that, too.[14]

The call to sit with our humiliation, to feel the pain of what it is to be the inheritors of whiteness as cherished property, an inheritance that justifies Trump's comments, and which cannot be divorced from Protestant Christianity, is the call I seek to follow. While the scope of this essay does not allow for a complete exploration of methods for such following, I want to offer two resources that might help us to sit better together with our guilt: the

---

13. Harney and Moten, *Undercommons*, 65.
14. Gay, "No One Is Coming to Save Us from Trump's Racism."

Asian concept of *han* as explicated by theologian Andrew Sung Park, and my own theoethic of "grave attending."

According to Korean American theologian Andrew Sung Park,

> Throughout its history, the church has been concerned with the sin of people, but has largely overlooked an important factor in human evil: the pain of the *victims* of sin. The victims of various types of wrongdoing express the ineffable experience of deep bitterness and helplessness. Such an experience of pain is called *han* in the Far East. Han can be defined as the critical wound of the heart generated by unjust psychosomatic repression, as well as by social, political, economic, and cultural oppression.[15]

If we are to prevent cycles of violence built through the unreconciled wounds of the victims of sin (in other words by *han*), Christian theologians must incorporate han into doctrines of salvation. It is not enough for the sinner to seek individual redemption from God; she must also seek restoration and justice for the one sinned against: she must address *han*.

Further, the concept of *han* amplifies the need to confront *systemic* sins. As Park clarifies through the work of Taiwanese theologian C. S. Song, "'[Han] is the rhythm of passion welling out of restless souls in the world of the dead, the wrongs done to them unrequited. Han is the rhythm of passion crying from the hearts of those who have fallen victim to social and political injustices.'"[16] When attentive to *han*, salvation does not simply recognize the role we sinners have had in the perpetuation of the woundedness of those we've sinned against (socially or individually), but rather marks, "a forward-moving event. [Salvation] is the actualization of potential. True healing takes place when people's potential, which has been blocked by han and sin, becomes free to be fulfilled."[17] In other words, a recognition of *han* calls us not only to mourn and care for those killed and debilitated by our "right" to whiteness as cherished property, but more so to dismantle such property rights altogether. The cries of hearts who have fallen victim to white Christian nationalism call us to tear down America's modes of racial exclusion and incapacitation so that we might clear the way for the flourishing of a truly beloved community.

To confront the *han* we've caused we must train ourselves to sit with the wounds. We must open ourselves to the moodiness of the wounded, to

15. Park, *Wounded Heart of God*, 10.

16. Ibid., 20.

17. Ibid., 107.

the "welling of passion out of restless souls." I name such an act of responsive witness "grave attending." Grave attending is a caring for the gravity, the pulling down to the material world, listening and feeling for what all its myriad emotions have to tell us, and where they have to lead us. Acts of grave attention refuse to efface the material mattering of others on the way to our own redemption. To gravely attend is to train the body and soul to welcome the penetration of lamentant cries, the cries of those who have been crucified by the construction of whiteness as cherished property. Because it is attendant to the damage of those that in the wake of our resurrective impulse we have let drown, grave attending is an art of living that does not rush toward individual or collective redemption out of the gravity of the damage done by the sin of whiteness. To resist such sinful resurrection, is to follow Gay and sit with the humiliation. It is to refuse cheap hope in favor of the solidarity needed to dismantle all the structures on which comfortable lies have been built.

The modes of witness offered by Park and myself do not request that we be frozen in shame. Our knowing that we as white people, and particularly white Christians, cannot be innocent should not lead to more impotence. Such witness does not pretend to see no difference between forms of Christianity that resist white supremacy and those that fortify it. Nor does such witness ignore the utility of pointing to ways Trump-style Christian nationalism conflicts with Jesus-centered living. Such witness asks us to sit with pain, to be humiliated, to be undone by the horror of what our people have built. Instead of individual or denominational or disciplinary pardon, let us be ungrounded, let us be responsible for the active dismantling of structures that have sheltered *all* white Christians for far too long.

7

Christian Kingship and the Empire's New Clothes

CLAYTON CROCKETT

Writer and scholar of religions Reza Aslan says that when his family left Iran and came to the United States, he embraced evangelical Christianity. For Aslan, author of the book *Zealot: The Life and Times of Jesus of Nazareth*, Jesus "was the central figure in America's national drama."[1] Aslan explains that he later abandoned Christianity when he discovered biblical criticism, and eventually returned to the "faith of his fathers," Islam. *Zealot* is somewhat controversial, but it makes a strong historical argument that Jesus viewed his mission in terms of an insurrection against the Roman occupation and the restoration of a divine kingdom of this world. Whoever Jesus was as a historical person, Christianity represents the assimilation of his gospel in terms of Gentile culture—Greek, Roman and then European and American. The European colonization of America in the name of Christianity means that the hemisphere is saturated with Christ, for better and for worse, as Aslan's identification of Jesus with America demonstrates. The insistence that America is the promised land bestowed on white Christians runs like a red thread throughout the history and identity of the United States.

Whatever Christianity is, if it possesses any essence, American Christianity is a perversion of it. In his important book *God Is Red*, Native American scholar Vine Deloria Jr. claims that, "In its practical sense, Christianity is a religion almost wholly determined by the culture in which it finds

1. Aslan, *Zealot*, xviii.

53

itself."[2] In the United States, Christianity serves primarily as a nationalist exceptionalism, allowing European immigrants to claim ownership over native lands and enslaved African peoples. During the 1960s and 1970s, this exceptionalism was bruised and battered by the civil rights movement and other liberation movements, including the American Indian Movement, as well as by the brutal assassinations of JFK, MLK, and RFK, by the scandal of Watergate, the oil shocks, and the prosecuting and outcome of the Vietnam War.

In 1969 a Republican strategist named Kevin Phillips published *The Emerging Republican Majority*, a book that envisioned a pact between Wall Street and the southern Christian whites alienated by Democrats' association with the civil rights movement. This majority emerged in the 1980s and grew during the 1990s and early 2000s under Reagan and two George Bushes. The Religious Right reaffirmed American Christian exceptionalism in the wake of the threats of minorities, liberals, and atheists to their way of life.[3]

The United States was becoming more authoritarian on the right to counter the perceived crises and anomie of liberalism on the left. This restoration of American identity was willing to compromise democracy to save the sovereign power of God and country. Freedom has become less the capacity of all people to participate in the political, economic, and social processes of the nation, and more the affirmation of the supreme value of America as the chosen nation of God, whose kingship we are neglecting.

Sovereignty is based on the democratic idea of popular or populist sovereignty, but in its recent form it flows from the top—starting with God and trickling down to the rich and powerful and finally to the unfortunate disenfranchised. This sovereign power is ultimately mediated by free markets as defined by corporate capitalism, but these markets are often considered to instantiate the invisible and providential hand of God, who steers the ship of America in a threatening and perilous world.

The high-water mark of recent American evangelicalism was 2004, when conservative Christians were seen as delivering the reelection of George W. Bush in a closely contested race with John Kerry. The latter part of the first decade of the twenty-first century witnessed a backlash against conservative Christian politics, along with the rise of a more militant

2. Deloria, *God Is Red*, 192.

3. Phillips later came to regret what he had helped strategize. See Phillips, *American Theocracy*.

atheism, represented by Sam Harris, Richard Dawkins, Christopher Hitchens, and Daniel Dennett. The repudiation of the Religious Right occurred during the global recession of 2008, and extended through the first term of Barack Obama.

Obama's historic election did not signify the promise of a postracial America but instead touched off a mutation of conservative identity expressed less explicitly in terms of religion and more in terms of race. White southern Christianity in alliance with the enormous financial resources of the Koch brothers and other wealthy Republicans formed the Tea Party to oppose Obama. The Tea Party was composed of mostly the same constituency as conservative Christianity, but here economic protests were highlighted over religious rationales, and racial issues, though still implicit, were given more scope to gestate in opposition to a black Democratic president.

The ongoing economic turmoil, where the stabilization of the economy postrecession simply restored the status quo, enriching the banks, the corporate elites, and the superrich, provides the backdrop for the election of 2016. Hillary Clinton represented business as usual, fending off a populist challenge from Bernie Sanders. On the Republican side, however, the populist candidate secured the nomination and upset the political norm. Donald Trump, despite his wealth and celebrity status, became the champion of an extraordinary protest against politics as usual.

The irony is that Trump, who fed into stereotypical prejudices against women, minorities, and liberals, is part of an administration that is dedicated to continuing the massive transfer of wealth from poor to rich over the previous few decades. America's original sin is twofold: the genocidal destruction of its native inhabitants, and the implementation of a system of race-based slavery to work profitable plantations. The United States was founded by a revolution against the king of England for the sake of liberty and freedom for wealthy planters, but slavery was retained and Indians were swept aside in the pursuit of more land for the spread of the empire. Eventually, the split between North and South over the extension of slavery to the western territories led to the American Civil War, and in the midst of that war President Lincoln issued the Emancipation Proclamation, a wartime measure to encourage southern slaves to revolt. At the conclusion of the war, the Thirteenth Amendment abolished slavery. The U.S. military shifted its goals from fighting the states that had seceded and turned to back to fighting the Natives on the plains and in the west, to make sure that either group could not prevent the growth of the country and the plundering of its natural resources in its expression of Manifest Destiny.

After Lincoln's assassination, the Radical Republicans pursued an agenda of Reconstruction of the Southern states, but it was resisted and eventually overcome by the end of the nineteenth century with the establishment of Jim Crow laws and segregation. Groups such as the KKK used terrorist means to enforce racial segregation, and it was not until after World War II that the civil rights movement flourished in the 1950s and 1960s. The efforts of activists, organizers, preachers, and radicals succeeded in getting the Civil Rights Act passed in 1964, partly due to the images showing the violence of segregationist societies.

The Civil Rights Act ended up driving many southern whites into the arms of the Republican Party, as Kevin Phillips had strategized. Meanwhile the Democrats, who embraced civil rights, were more defensive, because they had to reconcile their support of neoliberal capital with support of the people. The Democrats presented themselves as a labor party, but in fact they represented progressive social goals combined with regressive economic neoliberalism. The liberation movements of the late 1960s shook the world, but the economic shocks of the 1970s fundamentally transformed it. Around 1970, we reached a global inflection point in economic growth. The rate of growth continued to increase, but the rate itself began to slow. Widespread economic growth became incremental and more difficult to sustain.

The 1970s saw the first real awakenings to environmentalism, and the awareness of the critical situation of the planet in terms of limited resources. The Club of Rome published its famous report, *Limits to Growth*, in 1972. Domestic oil production in the U.S. peaked in 1970, and Richard Nixon was forced to abandon the gold standard in 1971, letting interest rates float free. In fact, the gold standard was replaced by a de facto oil standard, following the oil embargo of the U.S. by OPEC nations in response to the Yom Kippur War in 1973. The upshot is that as economic growth slowed, the only way to grow was relatively, both among and within nations. Over the last four decades, there has been an unbelievable concentration of wealth, and a corresponding impoverishment of millions of people. This concentration of wealth is driving the privatization of society, the dismantling of social welfare programs, and the elimination of taxes on capital and other assets.[4]

In the United States, the Republicans cynically appeal to religious faith and racial bigotry as they work with Wall Street to accelerate the transfer of wealth from the poor to the rich. The Democrats, in contrast, appeal to

---

4. For a sustained economic analysis, see Piketty, *Capital*.

a multicultural coalition of individuals but support economic and military policies designed to intensify neoliberalism. Both parties support the true sovereign of the country and the world, which is corporate capitalism. In the wake of the civil rights movement, both parties have helped establish what Michelle Alexander calls *The New Jim Crow*, which refers to the mass incarceration of millions of Americans, including a disproportionate number of blacks and minorities.

The American justice system pretends to be color-blind, but in fact it is not in its workings and its effects. Statistics show that all races use drugs at comparable rates, but blacks and other minorities are far more likely to be arrested, convicted, imprisoned and to serve on probation and parole than whites. According to Alexander, the war on drugs has contributed to "two-thirds of the rise in the federal inmate population and more than half of the rise in state prisoners between 1985 and 2000."[5] The Black Lives Matter movement is a response to the awareness of the how many young black males are killed by police officers in a context where the police claim that we live in a desegregated, color-blind society, but in fact blacks are far more likely to be stopped, harassed, arrested, assaulted, and shot. And most of the time the police officers are not punished because of the fears of black violence perpetuated on a fearful white America.

The election of Donald Trump is an intensification of these social and economic processes, even if it appears more extreme. More and more people are losing out in economic terms, and the result of the recession of 2008 creates nationalist and protofascist tendencies at the level of popular outrage. There is disgust with politics as usual, and for many people Trump represented a way to protest the system. In economic terms, he has continued the savage and hypercapitalist practices of the ruling elite, even as his governing style has been more of a spectacle. After the uprisings in 2011 of Occupy Wall Street, the Arab Spring, and the movements of the squares in Europe, we can detect a new emphasis on authoritarianism in global politics. Vladimir Putin's role in Russia is one instance, although he has been in power since the early 2000s, and he represents a return of nationalist order and power after the devastation of the breakup of the USSR. Xi Jinping has consolidated extraordinary power in China, although his authoritarianism is relatively softer, as China seeks desperately to continue its economic growth. Trump represents a more absurdist authoritarianism due to the spectacle of his administration, his behavior, his scandals, and his tweets.

5. Alexander, *New Jim Crow*, 60.

He may be challenging the conventions of politics, but he is practicing the same things that Kevin Phillips proposed in 1969, and appealing to the same populace.

Evangelical Christians know very well that Trump is not a Christian, but many support him nonetheless, because they claim that God put him into power for a reason, and Christians should follow Paul's admonition to the Romans to obey the current political rulers. God is using Trump to accomplish God's ends, which is to return America to its white Christian identity and to repudiate the idolatry of multiculturalism. Here kingship is not about a literal king but about seeing Trump as God's flawed but anointed vehicle for saving the USA from moral relativism and secular humanism. Sovereignty here is not a thing or a person but rather the *essential link* between corporate capitalism, American nationalism, and white southern Christianity in cultural terms. This is the link that must be undone, because it is destroying us.

We may think we worship God or Christ, when we really worship America—the money and power that the nation represents. Our faith in capitalism is a belief in the possibility of infinite growth, which is impossible with a finite amount of natural resources. We would need about four planets for every person to live at the material level of the average American, but we only have one. We are desperately searching for new ways to grow and thrive, whether with new technologies or a return to a lost past, a time when America was great before things went wrong. We want to know who to blame, and we hope that if we can defeat the terrorists, expel the immigrants, or stop the flow of jobs overseas, that somehow we can restore the American Dream.

The Dream is a nightmare. In fact, Trump appears less as a Messiah and more as a late-Roman emperor in his absurdity, infantile churlishness, and abuse of power. Trump is fiddling while America burns. The empire is on its last legs, clinging to its reputation and military might as it is surpassed by other forces and other forms. As a nation, we are locked into an economic system that is unable to confront the reality of resource scarcity. Corporate capitalism is based on a premise of indefinite it not infinite growth, and we are coming up against real limits to growth. We know this, but we desperately want to find ways to avoid facing it, so that we can continue to consume. Meanwhile the burning of fossil fuels is heating the planet and melting the ice in dramatic and irreversible ways.

An apocalyptic reckoning is nigh; but as Frederic Jameson states, and Slavoj Žižek repeats, it is easier for most of us to imagine the end of the world than the end of capitalism. American Christianity today serves its true master, promoting ignorance and demanding subservience to the demands of neoliberal capital. We want to believe that a god can save us, that there is a technological fix, or that somehow we will leave this planet for another one. These are all fantasies. All empires fall, including the imperial order of Man. As we thrash about, we are given more and more implausible scapegoats for our sin—the poor, the immigrants, the terrorists, the Muslims, the liberals, the media, the government. *Money Trumps All.* The good God is dead. Mammon reigns triumphant. But we have awakened the Dark Ones, the Chthonic gods. As Zeal and Ardor sings: "The riverbed will run red with the blood of the saints and the blood of the holy."[6]

---

6. Zeal and Ardor, "Blood in the River," *Devil is Fine* (MVKA Music, 2016). Thanks to John Wray for introducing me to their music.

8

Theological Resistance to U.S. Christian Nationalism

MARK LEWIS TAYLOR

U.S. CHRISTIAN NATIONALISM IS hardly a new threat. Moreover, this nationalism and the ways it shows itself in the phenomenon of Donald Trump's rise to the U.S. presidency are not the only threats, perhaps not even the greatest threats, of our time. I argue in this essay that Christian nationalism is best countered by resisting the U.S. imperium's corporate-warrior elite, an elite that continually prioritizes the corporate interests of a small percentage of U.S. population and then reinforces those interests with military force and presence abroad and militarized policing and surveillance at home. Theologically, resisting a corporate-warrior elite will require acknowledging and confessing the complicity of many of us in corporatized and militarized U.S. culture. The most important theological move, however, is our retrieval of a vigorous prophetic tradition that resists today's corporate-warrior elite as a structure of injustice and a repression of the poor that is destructive of both U.S. society and global well-being.

Towards a "Critical Report"

A truly "critical report" on Christian nationalism, then, does best to stress that this nationalism is a threat primarily *as it is part of* a larger threat. The argument stated above is meant to point to this more encompassing problem. This broader problem is what Enrique Dussel has theorized as a "prevailing system"[1] that services the "corporate warrior elite." Again,

1. Dussel, *Ethics of Liberation*, 215–17. See all of ch. 4, "Ethical Criticism of the

this elite works through brutal militarization and policing networks—within the U.S. and abroad, continually reinforcing interests, practices, and structures of neoliberal capitalism, white supremacism, and a hegemonic masculinism.[2] Together, these structures and interests make disposable the bodies of all the poor. These structures and interests especially attack, confine, and daily devalue black and brown bodies, bodies of poor women, bodies of those who do not conform to gender and sexuality norms, bodies of "other" religious adherents—especially Muslims; not to mention that the corporate-warrior elite also devalues weak or sick bodies and bodies with disabilities: indeed the elite devalues *any* persons who can be made subordinate or "other" to a prevailing system that celebrates or condones its interests. I am suggesting that the field over which imperial dominance and repression hold sway is the field in which also the "intersectionality"[3] of these many repressions, of these various discriminations and structured forms of violence systemically interplay and are played off against one another.

"From Ferguson to Palestine," as cried out by many of the best political movements of our time, marks the geopolitical space of suffering in our present political moment. "Resistance" today must inhabit and challenge the imperial geopolitics of U.S. domination "from Ferguson to Palestine" and at all points everywhere and in-between. The comprehensive nature of the challenge—even when we remain limited to local practices—calls forth a holistic and radical prophetic theology.

In an earlier book, *Religion, Politics, and the Christian Right: Post-9/11 Powers and U.S. Empire* (2005), I offered a description of this prevailing system, this U.S. corporate-warrior elite, within a broad vision of U.S. religion and politics. Those arguments were both political and historical. I will not replay those analyses here, though signs of that analysis will emerge in what I offer here.

The real challenge today is to keep to the fore this prevailing imperial system of U.S. corporate-warrior elites. I'm not sure that many in the so-called resistance to Trump are up to this. Many instead limit focus to issues of Trump's racism, to his misogyny or to his purported ignorance and lack of fitness for office. All these are worthy points of critique, but they fall short of what needs to be done. They fail to challenge the larger historical

Prevailing System" (215–90).

2. Haymes et al., eds., *Routledge Handbook of Poverty in the United States*, 1–2.

3. Crenshaw, *On Intersectionality* (forthcoming).

and political context of U.S. imperial drives for national and global sovereignty, and the repression and suffering that result from those drives.

Can We Criticize U.S. Imperialism? Will We?

Will the critics of Trump and Christian nationalism also critique the prevailing system of U.S. imperialism? Too often Trump's admittedly racist, atrocious, even dangerous antics and policies are decried while his opponents fail to criticize the aggrandizement of power economically and militarily that the U.S. exercises abroad. The primary examples are Democrats, whether in the name of Hillary Clinton or Barack Obama, who complain about Trump but then lose their voice in the face of U.S wars and corporate exploitation. The same Democrats who say they want to take down Trump because he's the worst thing they have seen are largely silent—certainly not effective for change—in the face of U.S mass incarceration at home and U.S.-enabled imperial devastation in Yemen, Honduras, Palestine, and other places. Liberals lament Trump's "shithole" language but fail to analyze and resist the U.S. policies that for years have opened up abysses of political suffering for other people and for "othered" societies, cultures, religions, and ways of life. Even so, the peoples at those sites of suffering find ways of fighting back with dignity and power expressed in everyday existence. It is precisely by forging real and effective solidarity with those peoples in struggle, *against* U.S. imperialism and its corporate-warrior elite that real resistance and a comprehensive prophetic theology might emerge, and by which real "critical" reporting and thinking can arise.

Who will take up *this* kind of resistance? Who will say, as Angela Y. Davis did at a 2016 conference on the "black radical tradition," that many of us need to let go of the solace and advantage we have found in a nationalist "allegiance to America." Davis intoned, "I know as black folks in the U.S. we have thrived on nationalism. But there comes a time when we have to let it go. We have to let it go."[4]

Davis's call is not an easy one to issue. It is not one that gets much traction in U.S. society, even among activists. This is so even when the worst of U.S. imperial wars are on display. Harvard philosopher William James, for example, supported anti-imperialist groups in criticizing the U.S. imperial war in the Philippines and gave voice to the problem in 1903:

4. Davis, "Police, Prisons and the Neoliberal State." See the video (https://www.youtube.com/watch?v=T6B6BFyGUIQ) at the 2:00:56 mark.

> *To the ordinary citizen the word anti-imperialist suggests a thin-haired being just waked up from the day before yesterday, brandishing the Declaration of Independence excitedly and shrieking after a railroad train thundering toward its destination to turn upon its tracks and come back. Anti-imperialism, people think, is something petrified, a religion, a thing that results in martyrdom, for which to 'discuss' means only to prophesy and denounce.*[5]

But for those who live on "the underside of history," as Dietrich Bonhoeffer is oft-quoted as saying, which means to live under the boots and prevailing systems of imperial formation, there is no luxury to dismiss anti-imperialist struggle as mere crazy-man talk. Counterimperial struggle is a resistance that daily life requires. The resistance was always there in revolts among African slaves whose forced labor in the Americas powered European capitalism and U.S. imperial formation. That resistance often forms as a persistent "quiet encroachment" among those exposed to imperial subjugation, as Asef Bayat argues in *Life as Politics: How Ordinary People Change the Middle East*. Studying quiet encroachment in Cairo, Bayat writes, "I am referring to the lifelong struggles of the floating social clusters—the migrants, refugees, unemployed, underemployed, squatters, street vendors, street children, and other marginalized groups whose growth has been accelerated by the process of economic globalization."[6] Such means of mobilization from ordinary and daily "quiet encroachment are the conditions for later and productive revolts, say, by Palestinians against the U.S.-Israel alliance or by Egyptians against U.S. imperial interests in Egypt. These are real-world occurrences or possibilities. Counterimperial struggles *do* exist. Granted, one can find crazed forms of anti-imperial cries. We should not forget, though, that as empires "overreach," and they nearly always do, the daily resistances can build toward revolt and exploit the fissures opening up when imperial powers overreach.[7] Revolutionary journalist Mumia Abu-Jamal gave voice to this hope-making truth when he wrote:

> *Conventional wisdom would have one believe that it is insane to resist this, the mightiest of empires, the victor in the Cold War, the empire that devastated Iraq and all that. But what history really*

5. James, "Philippine Question," 1132.

6. Bayat, *Life as Politics*, 46.

7. On the long tradition of subjugated but invisible peoples and their special techniques of resistance, see Gordon, *Hawthorn Archive*, 113–202.

shows is that today's empire is tomorrow's ashes, that nothing lasts forever, that to not resist is to acquiesce in your own oppression. The greatest form of sanity that anyone can exercise is to resist that force that is trying to repress, oppress, and fight down the human spirit.[8]

The process of erosion of U.S. empire has already begun. In the very process of explaining, in his lucid and thorough trilogy of studies of U.S. empire, former CIA analyst and historian Chalmers Johnson in fact documents "the end of the American Republic," viewing this end as a rising *Nemesis* against U.S. imperial policies.[9] The imperial U.S. will face, may already be facing, effective challenges to its global power and at multiple world sites. As Martin Luther King Jr. argued in 1967 with a force that has still gone unheeded by liberals, conservatives, and many architects of U.S. power, U.S. counterrevolutionary action and economic pursuits have put the country "on the wrong side of a world revolution."[10]

King prescribed an alliance of secular peoples of conscience with other peoples who could draw upon core essentials of love and justice that he saw uniting "Hindu-Moslem-Christian-Jewish-Buddhist belief."[11] Both King's diagnosis and his prescriptions have gone unheeded through to the current year, a time spanning more than fifty years and ten U.S. presidents' administrations (Johnson through Trump). The call for resistance to U.S. imperial policies of our corporate-warrior elite is long overdue. How we undertake this counterimperial task will depend, in part, on how we relate "Christian nationalism" to the entrenched U.S. imperial formations still at hand.

Christian Nationalism—What Is It?

It is important to say what precisely what we mean by Christian nationalism and how we understand its functioning. To repeat, we best name it and fight it when we understand how it relates to the "U.S. imperial" and its fusion of corporatist and war-making policies.

8. Abu-Jamal, "Interview with the *Revolutionary Worker*." On Abu-Jamal's extensive corpus, see Fernández, ed., *Writing on the Wall*.

9. See especially the third volume of the trilogy: Johnson, *Nemesis*, 10–11, 73, 242. The other two books of the trilogy by Johnson are *Blowback* and *Sorrows of Empire*.

10. King, "Time to Break Silence," 240.

11. Ibid. 242.

I take nationalism to be distinctive from patriotism, in that nationalism, as Anatol Lieven has noted, issues in more tumultuous outcomes. Nationalism often adds to "patriotism," which is the critical or uncritical "love of country," an aggressive programmatic edge. Lieven writes that nationalism has a "certain revolutionary edge" even a "messianic vision."[12] As I noted in a 2005 work during the rise of nationalism after the attacks of 2001 on the World Trade Center and Pentagon in the U.S., nationalist programs with their messianic dreams for the nation often concentrate power. They deploy force: They apply economic force in the form of expropriated labor and regressive taxation. Further, they apply social force by implementing brutal, blatant, and pervasive white racist practices; by curtailing citizen liberty; by instituting forms of martial law; and by promoting police and paramilitary violence, torture, and war.[13]

Nationalism can be "Christian" in at least two closely related forms. First, nationalist projects harness beliefs and sensibilities about God's providence, and this often leads Christians to rationalize and legitimize nationalist projects. Many U.S. Christian youth are homeschooled in this theocratic nationalism, and it circulates among Christians often in the highest corridors of U.S. national power.[14] There is of course a long history in the U.S. of such theocratic impulses. It undergirds a Christian American exceptionalism. An early and still fine treatment of this history can be found in Martin Marty's *Righteous Empire*.[15] Christian missionizing impulses have often been grafted onto American nationalism, interpreting the command of Christ to "Go therefore and make disciples of all the nations."[16] as religious justification for a "violent evangelism" that long has been endemic to U.S. and European colonizing enterprises.[17] In its second form, this Christian nationalism can also become "christocratic." Indeed, most calls for theocracy in the U.S. are calls also for christocracy.[18] Both

12. Lieven, *America Right or Wrong*, 6, and see 223n6.

13. Taylor, *Religion*, 44–45.

14. Balsiger, dir., *George W. Bush*.

15. Marty, *Righteous Empire*; see especially ch. 4, "Charter for Empire" (35–45) and ch. 8, "Command of Christ, Interpreted" (78–88).

16. Matt 28:13 (NASB).

17. Rivera Pagán, *Violent Evangelism*. Indeed, missionaries have occasionally also issued challenges and their own resistance to colonialism. See Memmi, *Colonizer and the Colonized*, 72–73.

18. See Alexander, *Christocracy*. On megachurch christocratic pastor, Rod Parsley, see Posner, "With God on His Side."

are dangerous, perhaps the latter more so since it involves raising U.S. Christianity to special status over other religions within the nation as well as abroad. That nearly 80 percent of U.S. white evangelicals[19] voted for "America first" Donald Trump (enough to make up 65 percent of his more than 95-percent-white voting bloc) shows how strongly the nationalist enterprise draws upon christocratic reflexes of American religion.

Christian nationalism, then, is a religiously sanctioned vision that affirms ruling elites' nationalist projects. Religion's legitimizing function is so powerful that even secular-leaning political thinkers can call for it in the name of effective state rule. Political philosopher Leo Strauss, for example, one of the revered thinkers of neoconservative politicians, prescribed strong doses of religion to cement the unity of the polis with a religiously sanctioned and aggressive nationalism.[20] Christian nationalism is a religio-political ideology that lubricates the U.S. imperium. The parts of the U.S. imperium's engine are rendered more smoothly operable by this ideology.

Let us not think that Christian nationalist ideology is the sole cause of American nationalism. One must also study widespread desires for greed and unlimited accumulation, the hubris behind the desire for global sovereignty, and white-supremacist structures. None of these can be reduced to Christian nationalism. Drive for "American greatness" is also fueled by other sources. Christian theologians, though, have the special task of developing methodologies and beliefs to deconstruct entrenched ideologies of Christian nationalism. In the next section I identify four tasks that may aid theologians in deconstructing Christian nationalism.

Challenging the U.S. Imperium—
Four Christian Theological Tasks

Four theological tasks can challenge the U.S. imperium. Each of the tasks identified here is distinctive, though not separate from one another. They not only overlap conceptually and practically, but the operations involved in each task reinforce the operations in the others.

19. Smith, "Among White Evangelicals."
20. Taylor, *Religion*, 67, 85–95. See also Drury, *Leo Strauss*, 148–49.

1. Acknowledge the Complicity of Christian Belief

Theologians need to continually expose the complicity of Christian beliefs as a centuries-long problem. Christian thought and practice have a long heritage of being at work in European colonialism and empire-building as well as in US imperial and neocolonial systems. Again, Trump's blatant and brutal language, however problematic, should not cause us to forget that this nationalism has often been displayed throughout U.S. history and by nearly all groups of its ruling elites. I don't need to belabor this well-established point here. In addition to Martin Marty's book *Righteous Empire,* there is Bruce Lincoln's *Religion, Empire, and Torture,* and David Chidester's *Empire of Religion.*[21] For those wanting a more theoretical explication of how colonialism and empire have for centuries built on European-led "Christianization," especially in the Americas, see Walter Mignolo's corpus of writings.[22] The point here should be a banal one: theologians cannot now afford to go silent on the long-standing as well as present-day complicity of Christian belief systems in supporting U.S. imperial policy of economic exploitation and military domination. Theologically, this is a site for acknowledgement, confession, and prophetic critique and resistance.

2. Disrupting the Rhetoric of the "Christian Nation"

Theologians need to break any sense of identity between Christian communities and ideals, on the one hand, and the U.S. nation's political and social forms, on the other. Relationships of similarity and analogy here may pertain, but not those of identity. Certain practices of the nation may approximate the love and justice of the kingdom of God (*basileia tou theou*), for example, but those practices can never be identical to it. The *basileia* ideal here especially needs to be conceptualized and practiced in ways that stress its counterimperial meanings for Christian faith. Such a faith means opposing and countering those nation-state agendas with imperial intentions and pursuits of global sovereignty. For example, the U.S. government's promotion, under the Pentagon of Bill Clinton's presidency, of a global practice of "full spectrum dominance" for the U.S. could be rendered as betrayal of the gospel and of the kingdom of God. Such dominance lifts up one nation to the status of ultimacy, as having "full spectrum dominance."

21. Lincoln, *Religion*; Chidester, *Empire of Religion*.
22. Especially Mignolo, *Local Histories/Global Designs*.

The hubris here is evident even in the name the Pentagon gave to its missile attacks on Afghanistan and on a pharmaceutical plant in the Sudan in August 1998: "Operation Infinite Reach." The point here, theologically, is to maintain a critical distance between functioning Christian beliefs and Christians' loyalty to nation, to resist sacralizing the nation. This may seem a banal point, especially to Reformed theologians informed by Karl Barth's talk, following Søren Kierkegaard, advocating an "infinite qualitative distinction"[23] between God and the world. Alas, even though their national leadership may have decried wars by the U.S. in Afghanistan and Iraq,[24] many Reformed churches lost the needed critical distance between loyalty to nation and loyalty to God. Nationalism was left unchallenged even as U.S. wars violated international law.[25]

3. Turning to "Empire-Critical Studies"

In order to break the identity of Christian social units with U.S. imperial formations, it is necessary that theology construe the core sacred narratives, biblical theologies and central Christian symbols with the aid of what has been called "empire-critical theory." Davina Lopez, a scholar of New Testament and early Christianity, foregrounds "empire-critical" theory in her work on the apostle Paul in Roman contexts. This "scholarship echoes a non-idealist agenda by its commitment to renewed and reconfigured historical analysis, recognition of the need to pay attention to imperialism ancient and modern, and a concern for transformation of social conditions."[26] Like Brigitte Kahl,[27] Lopez offers brilliant counterimperial readings of Paul that challenge the largely depoliticized and spiritualistic readings of Paul offered up by U.S-American churches, readings largely unchallenged by an often "depoliticized" biblical scholarship. Richard Horsley too has pointed out the problem of biblical and theological "depoliticization" of biblical texts and has himself led the way in calling for a measured and nonreductionist if also urgently propounded "repoliticization" of biblical and theological scholarship.[28]

23. Barth, *Epistle to the Romans*, 10.
24. Religion News Service, "Religious Groups Issue Statements."
25. Williams, "Dangerous Precedent"; Holmes, "Legacy of Fallujah."
26. Lopez, *Apostle to the Conquered*, 9.
27. Kahl, *Galatians Re-Imagined*, 209–44.
28. Horsley, *Jesus and Empire*. See especially the opening chapter, "American Identity

But still, too many Bible training centers, and in the highest echelons of theological education, continue to service a depoliticized Christian religion. This masks the gospel's counterimperial meanings, and thus Christianity is easily co-opted by the forces of U.S. imperial power—even if those very same scholars complain about Donald Trump's politics. A critical re-politicization of biblical scholarship can take place, and without the much-feared "reduction to political ideology." We await additional scholarship to take on the task, and even more we require Christian communities to live into a counterimperial politics of the gospel.

Christians claim to follow the figure of Jesus, who died on a Roman imperial cross, and who demands such a counterimperial faith. New Testament scholar Paula Fredricksen has argued that Jesus' crucifixion may be the one historical fact we can confirm about him. To follow a crucified figure, Jesus, is to find oneself thrown into a political struggle alongside those whom Ignacio Ellacuría termed "crucified peoples" of our current period.[29] That solidarity cannot help but be political. We also know historically that the cross was a particularly "miserable and shameful death" that the empire reserved for the threatening poor, the slave, the rebel—the politically inconvenient souls who transgressed political proprietors and leaders and their religious supporters.[30] Theologians who do not get political to resist empire's political and economic domination are hardly consonant with the gospel of a crucified Jesus. I say this in critique of not only conservative, "Christian Right" interpreters but also of respectable liberals who see themselves (ourselves perhaps) with a more urbane, sophisticated, probably "multicultural" affirmation of diversity against Trumpian ways.

4. Prayers and Practicing "Boycott, Divestment and Sanctions" (BDS) toward Israel

Allow me to close with two examples of counterimperial faith needed in our time and especially in U.S. communities. Both examples come from two long-standing personal concerns I have carried since the time of the Vietnam War; these concerns extend to today's U.S. wars in Iraq, Afghanistan, Libya, and Syria—and also to the U.S.-backed wars and covert war

and a Depoliticized Jesus," 1–14.

29. Ellacuría, "Crucified People."

30. See Cook, *Crucifixion in the Mediterranean World*, a major study, especially 358–79 and 418–30.

operations on nearly every continent.[31] My two proposals here are ways to give public voice to a Christian liberation politics of counterimperial faith.

First, I suggest that Christians in their churches *pray by name* for the peoples and groups that the U.S. has deemed enemies to the nation. During especially the U.S. assaults on Iraq in 1991 under George H. W. Bush and then again in 2003 under George W. Bush, I visited many a church seeking to hear a faith language in prayer or sermon that named the peoples on the receiving end of U.S. firepower, of U.S. "shock and awe" tactics. Usually I looked in vain. Like the major U.S. generals, who rarely count enemy dead, much less name them, U.S. Christians at best tend to abhor violence "on all sides" while lifting up prayers for "our soldiers" but rarely, if ever, pray for civilians and soldiers on the other side, and again rarely by name.

Prayer is a staple of religious piety, especially among U.S. Christians. Yet, an American captivity of prayer too often persists, confined to rhetorical observance of national boundaries. Many times I have penned a statement or essay critical of U.S. leaders and presidents because of the destruction they have meted out to other peoples, only to hear from a pious Christian: "Well, don't forget to pray for the president." Sure, okay, as a human being and creature sullied but still somehow made in the image of God, a U.S. president might deserve such a prayer. But you're not going to ask me to pray for the largely innocent civilian-victims on the other side, or for those among enemy soldiers caught up, as our soldiers are, in the brutal vicissitudes of military conscription and war?

If and when I go to pray as a Christian, am I not to be challenged to name the greatest scores of the slain simply because they are not U.S. dead? Yes, in most cases English speakers may have to work to pronounce the names of hosts of Asian, African, and Arabic persons on compiled lists.[32] To name these deaths at the heart of the pious practice of prayer might be one small way to start world peace against the U.S. imperium's addiction to war.

Second, I call for a necessary and concrete practice. Grasping its import requires our recalling that the militarily enforced "peace" of U.S. empire, Pax Americana, involves a number of crucial alliances. One such alliance is prominently underwritten by sacred narratives and particularly

---

31. Vine, "U.S. Probably Has More Foreign Military Bases"; also Lucas, "U.S. Has Killed."

32. For a list of Iraqi civilians killed by U.S. military operations, see Sloboda, "100 Names of Civilians Killed."

by Jewish and Christian biblical narratives. I refer especially to the U.S. alliance with Israel, constituting what comparative literature scholar and Palestinian activist Edward Said termed, a pax Americana-Israelica.[33] The problem with this alliance is not simply that by it the U.S. legitimizes and supports Israel's illegal occupation of Palestine[34] with nearly unparalleled military aid to Israel, in spite of a well-documented reality of Israeli-sponsored "ethnic cleansing of Palestine."[35] The problem is also that this alliance with Israel becomes a pillar of U.S. policies in the Middle East, pulling in other partners in alliance, such as Saudi Arabia and the Gulf oil states, so that these together then unleash destabilizing forces and war. One of the outcomes of all this is the flight of refugees from war-torn areas of Syria and Iraq into Europe and the U.S.[36]

I suggest that the time is long past due for the guilds of the American Academy of Religion (AAR) of the Society of Biblical Literature (SBL) as well as for U.S. Christian churches to collectively work toward endorsement of the Boycott, Divestment, and Sanctions (BDS) movement. The best arguments for that endorsement, I believe, are provided in a book by Omar Barghouti, *Boycott, Sanctions, and Divestment,* and at the website on the BDS movement's progress.[37] This is a boycott that is no mere product of "outside agitators" or well-meaning liberals. It has its origins in over one hundred grassroots organizations in Palestine itself. The Association of Asian American Studies was the first academic guild to endorse BDS, in 2013. The American Studies Association endorsed it later, also in 2013. Critical theorist Judith Butler has laid out additional helpful arguments for the BDS initiative in 2013.[38]

I suggest that U.S. Christians and churches, as well as scholars of the AAR and SBL where we are gathered for this occasion now, have a special obligation to weigh in on this imperial alliance, the pax Americana-Israelica. This is because of the ways sacred narratives are so regularly deployed to fuel the conflict and legitimize Israel's illegal occupation. Political theorist Achille Mbembe has made two important points pertinent to the

33. See, for example, Said, *Covering Islam,* xxxv.

34. For a meticulous analysis, see Finkelstein, "Is the Occupation Legal?"

35. See historian Ilan Pappé, especially Pappé, *Ethnic Cleansing,* 1–9.

36. On the relation between these various entities and "pillars" of U.S. policy in the Middle East, see Prashad, *Arab Spring / Libyan Winter,* 45–64.

37. Barghouti, *BDS.* For the BDS website, see https://bdsmovement.net/what-is-bds/.

38. Butler, "Judith Butler's Remarks to Brooklyn College."

Israeli-Palestine crisis. First, he has argued in his influential essay, "Necropolitics," that the organized occupation of Palestine by Israel with U.S. backing is "the quintessential example" of "late-modern colonial occupation." At such a site, where the most minimal standards for occupying forces are routinely violated, theologians should advocate for the dispossessed and brutalized peoples. Mbembe underscores his first point with a second one, noting that it is "sacral narratives of national identity that underwrite the state strategies of division and fragmentation" and that sustain late-modern colonialism.[39] Christians need to join with their Jewish and Muslim colleagues, and also with peoples of all faiths (and those of no formal religion) to deconstruct the way such "sacral narratives" dispossess and destroy the peoples of Palestine.

Unfortunately, in the U. S. strong Christian Zionist currents not only underwrite Jewish rights to life and peace (to be sure these must be guarded) but also justify Israel's usurpation of Palestinian lands and rule over Palestinian peoples. That the occupation is illegal in the eyes of international law and lays waste to nearly any semblance of life for Palestinian peoples rarely is a concern for these U.S. Christians. Liberal Christians, who often demonize the "Christian Right" for being "conservative" and staunch supporters of Israel, still often lose their voices when it comes to advocating specifically for Palestinians. They go PEP—progressive except for Palestine—as many activists say. This lack of advocacy points to widespread failure by U.S. churches. The churches often forgo advocacy for Palestine because they fear charges of anti-Semitism when criticizing Israeli policies. A church with truly counterimperial faith and courage will maintain a voice to criticize every form of anti-Semitism *even while* roundly condemning Israel's illegal occupation and destruction of Palestinians and their land. As I write, U.S. and Israeli leaders continue their denunciation of the BDS movement as straight-out anti-Semitic. In the United States efforts continue (even by many vociferously opposed to Trump) to pass laws against those of us in support of BDS.[40] Nevertheless, theologians of counterimperial faith in the age of Trump should take a stand in solidarity with Palestinians' own call for a policy of boycotting, divestment, and sanctions.

39. Mbembe, "Necropolitics," 11–40 (see 14).
40. *Electronic Intifada*, "Anti-BDS Laws."

CONCLUSION

The four theological tasks of the previous section are not the only ones necessary in this political moment. Nevertheless, begin with these four, and theology will not only be taking on Christian nationalism. It will also be challenging the U.S. imperium's corporate-warrior elite. We will not effectively deal with the threat of Christian nationalism without confronting the imperial interests of this U.S. corporate-warrior elite. This elite—not only its conservatives and neoconservatives but also its liberal hawks and urbane liberal academics—is what often creates and sustains the conditions for the possibility of Christian nationalism. The resistance must dare to challenge this elite.

PART 2

American Exceptionalism, Evangelicalism, and Trumpism

9

The Time of America

JOHN D. CAPUTO

We have chosen the expression "Christian nationalism" with a chip on our shoulder, to get in the face of the Christian nationalists—the phony nationalism of so-called Christians is what we mean. The expression drips with irony; it is accusatory, a term of abuse meant to expose something hypocritical, dangerous. This is a corruption of *Christian* and *nation*, which have fallen into the hands of people unworthy of these names, where they signify something ignorant, thoughtless, mean-spirited, angry, exclusionary, oppressive, reactionary. In theology, this is called blasphemy, a desecration of something sacred. We are gathered here to mock the mockery.

First as tragedy, November 8, 2016, then as farce, then as a circus, then as a sick joke—like using the gospel story of Joseph and Mary to justify child molestation. I hesitate to use a timely example, however applicable, because the stream of timely examples in Trumpworld, is so steady that examples become obsolete in a matter of hours. We can calculate their shelf life only with a stopwatch. We have a hard time keeping track of egregious offenses that would otherwise, in a time not so very long ago, be completely unforgettable, career ending. This is not normal; this must not become the new normal. This is not a paradigm shift; this is the implosion or explosion of the prevailing paradigm, pure and simple, with nothing to replace it. If, as Heidegger says, the sense of Being goes back to the sense of time, this is the sense of time in Trumpworld: where nothing is, and everything mutates; where even Heraclitus would begin to complain at the fast pace of the flux; where everything instantly evaporates in billowing clouds of confusion and contradiction, in tidal waves of deceit, denial and dissemblance, in a tsunami of twittering tweets. This is Kierkegaard's worst nightmare, a profusion of mediatized *Gerede*, of spurious, devious, misspelled duplicity, appealing to the base, the basest instincts of the base, the very worst instincts of the people. This is the corruption of the people, of "we the people," of the "people of God," of the *nation*. All this, God help us, in the name of Jesus, a name so badly abused, so defiled daily, that I prefer to say Yeshua, to decontaminate him from these so-called Christians.

In the blasphemous simulacrum that passes for *Christianity* on the Christian Right today, owning a gun is a right but having health care is a privilege; in the election of public officials, character matters, until it does not—until it serves the political interests of the Right to dismiss personal character, then it suffices to support a mendacious narcissist who brags about the obscene things he can do to women because he is rich and famous. In the blasphemous simulacrum that passes for "nationalism," these Christians rejoice in Christian militarism, just when Jesus said to put down their sword; when the Scriptures say to welcome the stranger, they dig in against the immigrants; they hold that bringing good news to the poor, feeding the hungry, and healing the lame is coddling people who are on the dole; if these particular "neighbors" whom Jesus asks us to love ever moved into their neighborhood—indeed if Jesus ever moved into their neighborhood—they would move out for fear that property values would go down. Instead of the Good News, Fox News. Instead of the year of the Jubilee, when all debts would be forgiven, instead of the condemnation of the rich in the New Testament, they support a tax cut that represents a massive redistribution of wealth to those who are already obscenely wealthy. When Jesus said, suffer little children to come unto me, they think that means depriving women with unwanted pregnancies of medical insurance, proper prenatal medical care, and throwing those little children and their mothers on their own after they are born, like Hagar and Ishmael. It is surely such Christians as these that Jesus would have spit out of his mouth.

A nation is an event of natality. *Nation* means the natal place, the natal community, the place we are born and the people by whom and among whom we have given birth. Our attachment to it is natal, natural. Such attachment is a fabric that is woven of all the lines of force of birth, all the corporeality and affectivity of familiar faces and places, of the childhood home, old friends, the old neighborhood, a gradually widening world which eventually embraces the national home and, increasingly, the global one, mother earth, which is the mother of us all. Birth is a matter of a gift we did not ask to receive, for which we are spontaneously grateful. The national is a primordial community, a primordial formation of the spirit; it is a natal language and literature, a spirit that inspires us with ideals and shapes a form of life.

In this regard, the American nation has a marvelous novelty about it. It both is and is not a natal community; it is also and intrinsically an "intentional" community, whose very "idea" is to welcome the immigrant, those who have been displaced from their natal place and are welcomed here in order that they may make a new place for themselves and their children. In just the way that, as Derrida says, a "democracy" is an autodeconstructive community, that is, one whose founding principle is to always expose those principles to public interrogation, to maintain their perpetually self-questioning reformability and deconstructibility, so the American "nation" is an autodeconstructive natality, one that maintains the instability of the very idea of natality, so that it can be the place of those who have lost their place, the place of the displaced. Such a nation of migrants, wanderers, and pilgrims, resonates with the biblical injunction to welcome the widow, the orphan, and the stranger, and to provide for a city of refuge.

So, these self-professed Christian nationalists subject us to two blasphemies, two obscenities, two sick jokes, two embarrassments—their so-called Christianity and this so-called nation.

But make no mistake. We have also chosen our title in order to congratulate ourselves. *We* are not under accusation, not accused of anything. We are throughout on the side of the angels. So, allow me to "flag" (may I use this dangerous word here?) the egregious mistake, both strategic and conceptual, that academic theorists and other learned despisers of religion on the Left have made in handing these two words over to the Right. This mistake that was not made in the past. It was not made by Martin Luther King, under whose leadership the civil rights movement was not merely *compatible* with, but was *driven*, deeply *inspired*, by the demands that are made upon us all by both the Christian gospel and by the very idea of America.

This mistake was not made by Richard Rorty, whose *Achieving Our Country* went viral on November 9, 2016, the day after the catastrophe, when someone posted a citation from this book which told the Left that it had been warned. Eventually, Rorty said—it was 1997—the abandoned trade unions and the blue-collar workers, the working white lower middle class, would tire of having their manners corrected by postmodern professors and elect a self-styled "strong man" who would pretend to speak for them and then proceed to undo forty years of progress on the left. *Achieving Our Country*—this title offends the ears of today's left—spoke of loving the *nation*, the one that says "give me your tired, your poor, your huddled masses yearning to breathe free, the wretched refuse of your teeming shore. Send these, the homeless, tempest-tossed to me, I lift my lamp beside the golden door!"

This America is not only a geopolitical entity but an idea, a prayer, a dream—the one King spoke of when he said that civil rights movement was "a dream deeply rooted in the American Dream," in which all of God's people will be free, where freedom will ring from every mountainside. Then, and only then, King said, "will America be a great nation." Great, not with the power of an army but with what Joseph Nye calls the "soft power" of an idea that lifts up the powerless, first not in military and economic force, but because there the first are last and the last are first.

Notice the temporal shift: King spoke of the day when America *will be* great, of *making* America great, but not "great *again*," which is the con job, Trumptime, the reactionary nostalgia, Fascist time, the dog whistle to white supremacy. King would not rebut this insidious nationalist slogan, as today's pandering politicians do, by saying that America has *always* been great. That, too, is hypocrisy, a cruel joke, blackmail. No nation founded upon European colonization, upon a near genocide of the indigenous people who already lived here, and that carried out this colonization on the backs of African bodies whom it dragged here in chains; which has put its poorest youth in harm's way for an unjust cause, first in Vietnam and then in Iraq; where then as today poverty and oppression stretch from sea to polluted sea—no such nation can dare say, with a straight face, that it has always been great. To all such nostalgia, to every such Fascist memory, King would oppose what Johann Baptist Metz calls the *dangerous memories* of the dead, of the lynching tree (James Cone). King said that it *will be* truly great and for the *first time*, so the greatness is the greatness of the *dream*, like the DACA "DREAMers" today, the dream of the *to-come*, so the "great" belongs to *prophetic time*, and is spoken in the adventive mode of the to-come. O my American friends, there is no America, not yet, but it is coming, if only we can make it come. Not a phony America but the true one—where the truth makes us squirm, puts us on the spot, in the accusitive as Levinas says—meant that it is up to us to make it come true.

America insists; it does not exist. Its existence is up to us.

The "I Have a Dream" speech is from beginning to end a speech about the time of the dream, the dream of a great *nation*, one that would be, in the depths of its national heart, responsive to the call of the prophets and the gospel, to the imperative to bring good news to the poor, the hungry, the imprisoned. King's speech dreams of the year of the *Jubilee*, which is a year not in calendar time but in prophetic time, which is the time of the heart, the time of hope, the time of the impossible, the time of the to-come.

If the Christian nationalism of the American Right is a *hypocrisy*, the message of the secular Left is *spirit*-less. It lacks a *prophetic* vision, which impassions the heart, and it lacks Rorty's and King's *national* vision, the "dream" of a "great nation." It lacks *Geist*, which I would translate here as "guts." In the face of the shameless charade of Christian nationalism, the Left lacks the guts to cite the prophets and to dream of the year of the Jubilee when America will for be a great nation. For the *first* time.

10

Trump: The Apotheosis of American Exceptionalism

MICHAEL S. HOGUE

Trump and Theopolitics of American Exceptionalism

There have been and will be a multitude of analyses of how and why Donald J. Trump was elected president of the United States in 2016. The reality is that a confluence of many dynamics contributed to the outcome—from the strategic misinformation spread through Russian "active measures" to white racial resentment and evangelical Christian cultural retrenchment; from the xenophobic scapegoating of Muslims and refugees to the conspiratorial hatred of all things Clintonian; from the false equivalencies of mainstream news to social media's monetizing of cognitive bias; from Republican voter suppression and gerrymandering to Democratic infighting and the left's protest votes and nonvotes.

And yet, as unexpected as the election of Trump was for many of us, and as complex as the contributing causes may be, it should not have been a surprise. For Trump is the apotheosis—the deification and, perhaps, the denouement—of the long-standing tradition of American exceptionalism.

American exceptionalism is a distinctive alloy of Christian eschatology, white ethnonationalism, democratic missiology, capitalist triumphalism, and imperial hubris. Although the concept of American exceptionalism is frequently invoked, it is not often analyzed as a form of political theology. This is due in part to the American inclination to think of the political in purely secular terms. But neither the secular nor the political, whether in the United States or elsewhere, are theological vacuums. As famously articulated by Carl Schmitt, the godfather of modern political theology, "All significant concepts of the modern theory of the state are secularized theological concepts not only because of their historical development— in which they were transferred from theology to the theory of the state, whereby, for example, the omnipotent God became the omnipotent law-giver—but also because of their systematic structure."[1] In other words, the story of Western modernity, in which the emergence of the secular nation state is a pivotal chapter, has a theological plotline. It is the story of how an all-powerful God who transcends good and evil and determines justice is transubstantiated into an all-powerful state (or, in our time, a market/state) defined by its monopoly on violence and its capacity to constitute, surveil, and, when it wills to do so, suspend, the rule of law.

This generic theory of political theology is illuminating in many ways, but American exceptionalism is not merely the effect of transferring classi-cally theistic ideas onto a concept of the state. Rather, American exception-alism is fundamentally a Christian nationalist political theology, oriented by what I refer to as the "redeemer symbolic."[2] The redeemer symbolic grounds the moral logic and justifies the historical effects of American exceptionalism. By asserting that Trump is the apotheosis of American exceptionalism, I am making two claims about his standing in relation to this redeemer symbolic: first, that Trump the person represents, in his own mind as well as for his followers, a deification of the redeemer symbolic (apotheosis, as in made into a god); and second, that the Trump presi-dency could become, if "we the people" will it to be so, the denouement of the redeemer symbolic (apotheosis, as in climax, culmination, or crisis point). In what follows I will first define the theological structure of the redeemer symbolic before briefly outlining how it has functioned through the history of American exceptionalism. I will then discuss how resistance to the Trump regime may be inspiring a shift of theopolitical paradigms, from the redeemer symbolic to a more resilient and radically democratic countertradition.

---

1. Schmitt, *Political Theology*, 36.

2. For much more on this concept, and the development of a constructive alternative to it, see Hogue, *American Immanence*.

The Structure, History,
and Deification of the Redeemer Symbolic

The root metaphor of the redeemer symbolic is christological, but it migrates across diverse registers of meaning and across diverse periods in American history, and in all of them it sanctifies the moral structure of American exceptionalism. It affirms that there is one who (or that) is invested with exceptional saving power—the power to make right what is wrong, to bring order out of chaos, and to establish justice where there is lawlessness. This saving power is figured in various ways through American history—for instance, as the purifying church, the missional nation, or the free market. Though the focal figure may change, its saving power is ontologically singular. God or nation or the free market is a "one of a kind" that transcends the limiting conditions, moral, material, and otherwise, that constrain all other things of its class—other gods and religions, other races and nations, other forms of economy. An ideal of unitary, sovereign, invulnerable power pervades the redeemer symbolic—that which has the power to redeem is omnipotent, omniscient, and impassible. This ideality of power sanctifies the concentration of power and cultural, financial, and political capital, while its oppositional logic, grounded in the totalizing nature of its unitary structure, aids and abets American religious and political absolutisms.

In its early, ecclesial phase, the redeemer symbolic was formed out of the Puritan eschatological imaginary. Mirroring the Christian interpretation of the plot structure of the biblical story of exodus, Divine Providence, working through Puritan witness, would purify the church and thereby redeem the nations of the world. The sovereign agent of redemption, the Providential God, would save those who were obedient to his purposes and damn those who were disobedient. During this period, covenant was the medium of redemption, binding together a transcendent, exceptional God with his exceptional, chosen people. This ecclesial phase of the redeemer symbolic formatted a radically patriarchal and class-stratified theocratic culture in which magistrates and ministers exerted their divinely sanctioned power over all but God. Conformity was prized above all other concerns. Despite their Christian piety, dissenters such as Roger Williams and Anne Hutchinson were banished from Massachusetts. The threat of externalization became a tool of social order.

At the same time, the theft of land from native populations was theologically legitimated through the redeemer symbolic's trinitarian logic of exception, extraction, and externalization. This logic also justified the plundering of black lives, whose slave labor was the source of the capital that fueled the rise of the United States as an economic power. In the nineteenth century, the Puritan eschatological idea of redemption was transformed into the ethnonationalist doctrine of Manifest Destiny. Although the theological and political registers of the redeemer symbolic were transposed during this nationalist phase, its inner moral structure functioned in much the same way. The mantle of national and racial chosenness justified territorial expansion, the displacement and slaughter of hundreds of thousands of Native Americans, the terror of the plantation economy, and a transparently imperial war with Mexico. Through the doctrine of Manifest Destiny, the redemptive medium of Puritan covenant was converted into claims of Anglo-Saxon racial superiority, democratic missiology, and imperial expansion. In place of the sovereign, Providential God of Puritan imagination, the power to redeem was embodied within a white supremacist form of republican democracy.

Later, the rise of American industrialism brought about a new, economic form of the redeemer symbolic. Neither God nor nation, neither church nor state, but the free market had become the sovereign force of redemption, and capital was its medium. The omniscience of the market and the myth of economic meritocracy guaranteed that the winners earn and deserve their winnings, losers their losses. Wealth and poverty became metrics of moral worth. Over time, belief in the omnipotent market and its justice set the stage for the emergence in the late twentieth century of the neoliberal form of the redeemer symbolic. Within the neoliberal imaginary, the rights of life, liberty, and the pursuit of happiness asserted in the Declaration of Independence are converted into the dogmas of deregulation, privatization and free trade. What began with the Puritan errand to redeem the world by purifying the church, and then took shape as a racialized form of republican democracy, is now expressed through the global missiology of American capitalism. Now, the way to redemption is through a deregulated market, corporate tax cuts provide the keys to the kingdom, the government is the whore of Babylon, and affluence is a sign of righteousness.

When interpreted through the lens of the redeemer symbolic, the election of Trump represents less of a break with American political tradition and more of a fulfillment of its late capitalist, neoliberal phase. As one journalist observed immediately after the election, Trump is approaching the presidency "in the spirit of a tycoon making a new acquisition, overseeing the merger of Trump Inc and America Inc—a merger in which it is far from clear which would be the senior partner."[3] This early observation has been confirmed in the months since by the weekly golf outings and weekend getaways, the nepotism in the staffing of the White House, the appointment of billionaires and corporate executives to the cabinet, and the self-dealing in the tax legislation passed at the end of 2017. Like the mythology of the redeemer symbolic, Trump is a figment of his own imagination. He is a fetish to himself and a totem for his followers. He gives life to spurious worlds of alternative facts. He embodies the exception to the rule of law (thus far). And, in keeping with American economic tradition, he has made his fortune on the backs of others, outsourcing labor, leveraging debt, defaulting on loans, declaring bankruptcy, and refusing to pay his contractors.[4] In claiming that he alone can fix things, Trump is the redeemer symbolic grotesquely deified.[5]

The Denouement of the Redeemer Symbolic and the Rise of Resilient Democracy

The question that remains concerns the other meaning of *apotheosis*: can the Trumpian deification of the redeemer symbolic be turned into its denouement? The answer to this question can only be enacted—it is up to us, "the people," to decide. One thing, however, is clear. The crudity of Trump and the chaos and cruelty of his administration are causing an equal and opposite force to awaken—the emergent power of collective resistance. The paradox is that this collective power of resistance is being brought to life by a shared sense or a common feeling for the vulnerability of democracy. This paradox is a good sign, for becoming aware of the vulnerability of democracy, recognizing that it can be lost, is critical to the work of building a more radical and resilient democracy.

Encounters with vulnerability have a revelatory way about them. They bring focus to the mind and resolve to the heart and spirit. The awareness

3. Boger, "'Recipe for Scandal.'"

4. Among many other accounts of his business and personal failures, see Durgin, "Definitive Roundup."

5. For the full text of Trump's speech, accepting the nomination of his party at the Republican National Convention, see *Politico*, "Full Text."

of vulnerability, whether it is the deep feeling for one's own bodily vulnerability or the vulnerability of the ideal of a democratic body politic, is conscientizing. As such it compels a heightened state of perceptual and affectual awareness and spiritual and moral vigilance. The sense of vulnerability leads us to become more observant, and when this sense is shared, or experienced in common, it can lead us to feel more deeply our relations to others and to the wider world. This sense of vulnerability focuses our commitments to what we value, deepens our sense of responsibility, and widens our sense that we are a part of something much larger than ourselves. Encounters with vulnerability awaken us to the precarity of those relations and ideals that we value most, and they compel us to take up the work we must do, from wherever we are, to preserve and sustain those relations and ideals.

Many of us are more finely attuned to our civic relations and are re-committing to democratic ideals and habits in response to the common feeling that the American democratic experiment is more vulnerable now than it has been in generations, perhaps as far back as the Civil War. This is evidenced by the political activation of millions of formerly apolitical, civically disengaged citizens; by the numerous mass mobilizations of environmental and social justice activists, such as the record-breaking Women's March and the People's Climate March; by the rise of new grassroots democratic movements, including the thousands of Indivisible and 350 climate justice groups organizing in communities across the nation; by new crowdsourced modes of resistance, such as the thousands of Sleeping Giant activists using digital and social media platforms to get businesses to cease abetting far right propaganda with their advertising dollars.

Thus, it may be that the Trump presidency is just what American democracy has needed. To say this is not to endorse or deny the real harm the Trump regime is doing. Lives are on the line, especially queer lives, black and brown lives, poor and working-class lives, undocumented lives, and Jewish and Muslim lives. To say that Trump may be just what American democracy has needed is to say that Trump's flagrant disdain for democratic norms and institutions; his verbal and legislative assaults on immigrants, refugees, and Muslims; his decimation of civil rights and environmental protections; and the unreservedly ethnonationalist branding of his MAGA bluster may be the rude wake-up call that some Americans, too many of us, have needed to jolt us from our democratic slumber.

This awakening of the power of the people, brought about by a common feeling for the vulnerability of democracy, is what a more radical, resilient democracy demands. A more radical, resilient democracy is what is needed to resist the many powerful countervailing forces, deified by Trump and exemplified by the redeemer symbolic, opposed to democracy in our time. Building more resilient democratic communities to sustain democratic struggle requires that we recognize democracy's vulnerability; and recognizing democracy's vulnerability entails rejecting every claim to democracy's fulfillment.

A resilient democracy is one in which the people know, deep down, that the struggle for democracy is unending, that there is no utopian transcendent reality that is "democracy fully and finally realized." Indeed, the idea that democracy is vulnerable is essential to the very possibility and practice of democracy. As political theorist Sheldon Wolin has said, "The experience of which democracy is the witness is the realization that the political mode of existence is such that it can be, and is, periodically lost."[6] Our realization of this witness in this moment should motivate us to occupy the democracy that remains and to extend and enliven it by practicing it more fully in our everyday lives. For it is at the grassroots, in our local spaces, where the personal and social, the economic and the ecological, the spiritual and moral, and the planetary and political conditions of life are simultaneously most vibrant and most vulnerable. And we must be more fully attuned to the vibrancy of these conditions of life in order to have the courage to resist more vigorously those antidemocratic forces in the world that render them, and therefore all of us, more vulnerable.

6. Wolin, *Fugitive Democracy and Other Essays*, 111.

11

Foxangelicals, Political Theology, and Friends

CATHERINE KELLER

In December 2017, with the forty-fifth president trumpeting at political rallies that "Christmas is back, better and bigger than ever before," an eye-opening op-ed appeared in the *New York Times*. It bore the title "America's New Religion: Fox Evangelicalism."[1] Its author, Amy Sullivan, writing as a progressive evangelical, makes a confession that many progressive theologians (including those of us far from evangelical) may share: "Journalists and scholars have spent decades examining the influence of conservative religion on American politics, but we largely missed the impact conservative politics was having on religion itself."

What impact of politics on religion, distinct from the effect of religion on politics, did we miss? In the interest of a politically responsible reading—and so perhaps even practice—of religion, I want to stage that impact as an urgent matter for current political theology. For I suspect that the current impact of conservative politics will register as an intensification of an old dynamism, key to political theology, of friends versus enemies.

To track the dynamics of the current, however, poses quite a challenge to any writing that is off the fast track of journalism. How, on the schedule of a book, do we even name the current, the now, even an "age"? The "age of Trump," announced as the "threat of Christian nationalism," has well and swiftly mobilized the present conversation. We may resist ceding an age to the name of Trump. And we may question whether the

1. Sullivan, "America's New Religion."

89

category of nationalism is adequate to the contemporary convergence of white supremacism, transnational capitalism, rabid masculinism, and climate denialism. Does this nationalism's "Christianity" clinch the category? Surely not. But the point lies not with (my) tired righteous incredulity at the hypocrisy of a Christian right salivating over a foul-mouthed bully who barely bothered with "Christian" signals beyond the nonbiblical abortion button—however well he embodies the answer to the question, as Sullivan nails it, "What would Jesus not do?'" (WWJND!).[2] Let us rather consider whether political theology, in its progressive voice, can be of help in assessing—and so disclosing, *now*—what Sullivan calls "America's new religion." That is not a nomenclature that fits readily under the heading of Christian nationalism. But neither, as I think will become clear, does it contradict it.

The Political *Saeculum* on Religion?

Political theology traditionally analyzes the secularized effects of religion on politics. But does it go the other way to expose the effects of the political *saeculum* on religion? At the historic core of what is called political theology operates the proposition of the German jurist Carl Schmitt that "all significant concepts of the modern theory of the state are secularized theological concepts."[3] For Schmitt, this fact is exemplified above all by the notion of sovereignty, derived from the doctrine of divine omnipotence. It imports not just the sense of dominion—the divine right of kings—but of miraculous intervention. He notoriously pits "the miracle" against the boring bureaucratism of bourgeois liberalism. And he is arguing not for but against the socialist alternative. He attributes the threat of communist revolution in his context largely to the impotence of democracy, particularly that of the Weimar Republic between the wars. Then in his 1929 classic, *The Concept of the Political,* he posits that "the specific political distinction to which political actions and motives can be reduced is that between friend and enemy."[4] Brushing off the Christian counterposition, he insists that the biblical injunction to "love the enemy" has nothing to do with political

---

2. WWJD, the acronym popular among evangelicals, comes from *What Would Jesus Do*, the subtitle of Charles Sheldon's 1896 *In His Steps*, a popular novel developed through his preaching and his commitment to Christian socialism. For its hip reprise, see Caputo, *What Would Jesus Deconstruct?*

3. Schmitt, *Political Theology.*

4. Schmitt, *Concept of the Political*, 26.

enemies: "It certainly does not mean that one should love and support the enemies of one's own people."[5]

That exegesis immediately clears the politically theological way to Schmitt's definition: "The political is the most intense and extreme antagonism, and every concrete antagonism becomes that much more political the closer it approaches the most extreme point, that of the friend-enemy grouping."[6] Schmitt defines "the enemy" as "the other, the stranger; and it is sufficient for his nature that he is, in a specifically intense way, existentially something different and alien."[7] The enemy need not be mounting an attack or threatening a war. One grasps how such logic would come to support the production of "the Jew" as unifying enemy. For if the political collective comes down to oppositional identity, the religioracialization of a racial-ethnic other becomes the most effective means to essentialize at once an enemy. And therefore, as its immediate effect, our friends, the *we*.

Even in diametrical disagreement with Schmitt's politics, one may yet grant the widely applicable descriptive credibility of this account of politics. Or at least of an antidemocratic style of politics, with its hidden theology of autocratic power. Its use of fear and loathing to the end of unifying an "us" against a "them" found its extreme form, and Schmitt's approval, in the fascism of the 1930s. Eighty years later, anti-immigrant right-wing movements have been winning long-unthinkable parliamentary representation in Europe.

In this present tense, the United States victory of an "us" unified against unwhite others, both internal and immigrant, is not simply nationalist. Rather, it symptomatizes a disturbing international haze of nationalist antagonisms, calling to mind Hannah Arendt's eerie *post*war warning of the role that "white supremacism" would have in fomenting a new "fascist International."[8] So we (the invitational *we* of this essay, not the Schmittian *wir*!) face now what William Connolly calls, in his rapid response to "the age of Trumpism," an "aspirational fascism."[9] This notion builds upon his earlier analysis of the politics of antagonism, enabled by the festering resentment—the "ethos of existential revenge"—that had earlier given rise to "the capitalist-evangelical resonance machine." Drawing on the Deleuzian

---

5. Ibid., 29.
6. Ibid.
7. Ibid., 27
8. Arendt, "The Seeds of a Fascist International," in *Essays in Understanding*, 140–50.
9. Connolly, *Aspirational Fascism*.

figure of machinic assemblages, Connolly had proposed his resonance-machine in particular relation to the early twenty-first-century American intensification of right-wing Christianity as it coils together in a "state-capital-Christian complex."[10] This assemblage, always economically embedded, runs not just from religion to politics but circulates also from politics to religion. Its ability to unify significant portions of an economically disaffected working class with the superrich is an effect of their resonating together: "The bellicosity and corresponding sense of extreme entitlement of those consumed by economic greed reverberates with the transcendental resentment of those visualizing the righteous violence of Christ."[11]

The *they* may shift—divergent caricatures of racial or of religious difference come into play. But the unifyingly divisive strategy of antagonism persists in any event. And it has now dangerously intensified. This cannot be accounted for in terms of a unilateral operation of conservative or apocalyptic theology upon politics. There seems to be a circulation between the impact of religion on politics and the impact of politics on religion, indeed a cycle vicious enough to produce a change, as Sullivan hints, of religion. Or of the meaning of religion. Does this circulation express the unifying antagonism that we face in the currently manifesting dynamics of Christian nationalism?

"Us" versus "Them"

What Sullivan has found in her investigation of the overwhelming white-Christian-evangelical support for Trump is a significant change in the character of the religious right itself. And it registers precisely in the versatile politics of us vs. them. She interviews Reverend Jonathan Martin, a popular evangelical pastor and author: "It's meaningful, Mr. Martin says, 'that scions of the religious right like Jerry Falwell Jr. are not pastors like their fathers. There was a lot I didn't agree with him on, but I'm confident that it

10. Connolly, *Capitalism and Christianity*. He builds here on "Marx's insight into assemblages between private life, embedded spirituality, and the state." So he marks the "point at which Weber and Marx meet. For the mature Marx never did isolate a set of tight contradictions of capitalism; and . . . the ethos of Protestant Christianity incorporated into early state-capitalism was strongly disposed to blame poverty upon the character of the poor. Marx intimates in 'The King of Prussia' how capitalism the state and Christianity are intercoded to a significant degree, with a change in any finding some expression in the interior of the others" (ibid., 21).

11. Ibid., 48.

was important to Senior'—Jerry Falwell—'that he grounded his beliefs in Scripture,' Mr. Martin said. 'Now the Bible's increasingly irrelevant. It's just "us" versus "them.""

What medium has wrought such a bluntly Schmittian metamorphosis? Both Testaments could always be deployed in support of political antagonism: "if they are not for us they are against us."[12] But it would seem that, among avowed evangelicals, biblical attestation has dropped precipitously. There remains then no basis for the "whoever is not against us is for us" pushback![13] Indeed, a recent survey reports the startling finding that fewer than half of those who consider themselves evangelical actually hold traditional evangelical beliefs.[14] Among white "self-identified evangelicals," the label *evangelical* now functions, it seems, more as a cultural than as a theological identification. (African Americans, by contrast, are more likely to reject the term *evangelical*, apparently for its cultural whiteness, and yet to hold the biblically based beliefs.) Race and political party appear more likely than religious beliefs to determine how one votes. If, as Sullivan puts it, "*evangelical* effectively functions as a cultural label, unmoored from theological meaning," what then gives shape to the particular friend/foe binary that takes the place of biblical belief within evangelical identity?

This is where Fox News—and friends—comes into play. Sullivan led with the example of "the War on Christmas," a longtime Fox News campaign. It was never a religious argument (about, say, the virgin birth, or saving Christmas from commercialization):

> In an irony appreciated by anyone who remembers the original anti-consumption, anti-Santa meaning of the 'Reason for the Season' slogan, Fox and allies like the American Family Association focused on getting more Christmas into stores and shopping malls. These days, even though Mr. O'Reilly declared 'victory' last year [after the election] in the War on Christmas, Fox News still gives the supposed controversy wall-to-wall coverage and has folded it into the network's us-versus-them nationalist programming. The regular Fox News viewer, whether or not he is a churchgoer, takes in a steady stream of messages that conflate being white and conservative and evangelical with being American.[15]

---

12. Matt 11: 30.

13. Mark 4:40.

14. Smietana, "Many Who Call Themselves Evangelical."

15. Sullivan, "America's New Religion."

Note that the triumphant conflation of conservative Christianity with capitalism depends for its political force on the affective field of white supremacism, what Connolly calls an "affective contagion."[16] This constitutively American antagonism, with its dark foes—intimately African American, oscillating with intrusions Muslim or Mexican—proves indispensable in firing up the new "friends" of Christian nationalism. After all, it was on Fox News that we were reassured that not only was the historical Santa white like snow but "Jesus was a white man too."[17] The mouthpieces come and go, the issues flicker and shift. But as the primary purveyor of this political 'we,' conveying its daily charge of affective imagery, Fox News seems to be delivering the new political theology. It is taking the place of traditional beliefs for that majority of self-identified evangelicals, who no longer study the Bible. "A pastor has about 30 to 40 minutes each week to teach about Scripture," notes Rev. Martin. "They've been exposed to Fox News potentially three to four hours a day." Hence "Fox Evangelicals." Call them *Foxangelicals* for short.

The result, Sullivan suggests, is a "malleable religious identity that can be weaponized not just to complain about department stores that hang 'Happy Holidays' banners, but more significantly, in support of politicians like Mr. Trump or Mr. Moore—and of virtually any policy, so long as it is promoted by someone Fox evangelicals consider on their side of the culture war." She was especially stunned by the absolute importance of gun rights to most Fox friends. Here the primacy of antagonism comes blazing to the fore.

The documentary film *The Armor of Light* testifies to the new fusion of guns with God. Its protagonist is another thoughtful evangelical leader, Rob Schenk, earlier a popular pro-life crusader. We watch him run into one long wall of resistance when he begins to teach his constituency that pro-life values require restrictions on gun access. He finds that his public has been daily and successfully taught by Fox that their way of life, indeed their life, is threatened by terrorists, immigrants, (black) criminals, killers everywhere gunning for them. For Foxangelicals, gun ownership trumps the biblical teachings of respect for strangers, love of enemies, and welcome

16. Connolly, *Aspirational Fascism*, 15–16.

17. This is, of course, the then–Fox News reporter, Megyn Kelly, in 2013: "Just because it makes you feel uncomfortable doesn't mean it has to change, you know?" she said. "I mean, Jesus was a white man too. He was a historical figure, that's a verifiable fact, as is Santa—I just want the kids watching to know that." Quoted in Hadas Gold, "Megyn Kelly."

of aliens, as in Deut 10: "Love the foreigner, for you were once a foreigner in Egypt."

Taking the "Christian" out of the "Christian Right"

If it is true that Foxangelicalism has mounted something like a *"new* religion," it can never admit as much. That would take the "Christian" right out of nationalism. So we see here the potent effect of conservative politics upon religion. It functions by conveying a loud, new religioeconomico-political assemblage in which the biblical theology that justifies the 'we' has been—amid all the noise—quietly secularized. Very quietly, in fact, as secularism is something the right needs to accuse the left of. But this is a secularism that poses as religion, and indeed functions as a new one. John B. Cobb Jr. has long distinguished between the secular, to which he counts most major "religious" breakthroughs, and "secularism," which is its own religion. But he is referring to an atheist secularism, derived from modern liberalism and science. If Foxangelicalism can be called a new religion, it is the religion of a conservative secularism that masks itself as traditionally Christian and decries the secular (as waging, for instance, the war on Christmas).

It was after all as a theorist of the right that Carl Schmitt was exposing the secularization of theology in all forms, conservative and otherwise, in and through the modern state. He meant to make a conservative Christianity more directly effectual upon and within the political. The Schmittian political theology has been, since the world wars, perhaps more apparent in the United States than anywhere in Western Europe. Through the Reagan amalgam of a new religious right with the Republican Party, it produced the political resonance machine of fundamentalism and capitalism. But it now becomes evident that its impact goes deeper than the 'beliefs' of conservative Christians; indeed it goes to the root of evangelical—which is to say, biblically authorized—religion. And, covertly, it roots it out.

The machinic character of the assemblage, we suggested, does not work one way—from religion to politics. It circulates: from politics back upon religion. The politics is ouroborically swallowing its own religious tail. I would probably call the substitute a new megadenomination rather than a new religion, which suggests a misleading supersession of Christianity itself. Christianity remains, as ever, endlessly multiple and self-contradictory. But in its guise of sovereign supersessionism, is it itself being superseded?

Or rather is it not justifying the deep secularization of its most exclusionary we-they legacy? But it is certainly a new form of (its) religion. And so a supersession of the biblical—indeed evangelical—basis of Christianity.

Foxangelicals, now freed of the evangel itself, may be fully shielded from biblical debate and resistance. Therefore they cut free of the faint, lingering authority of biblical arguments coming from the prophets of social justice, from the gospels of public love, from the acts of agapic communism, from the radical Christians—Saint Paul to MLK Jr., Saint Francis to Pope Francis, Quakers to queer Christians. And such Christian antecedents of progressive politics can be over and over left in the dust. Antagonism, it seems, binds more efficiently than love; it provides a more politically unifying force of identification and belonging. At least temporarily.

Aspirational Fascism

Connolly shows how crucial to the current political condition is the "affective contagion" of its antagonism. He argues not that Trump is a Nazi—also not a bumbling idiot—but the "relatively skilled rhetorician of a new aspirational fascism."[18] Its political potency spreads through rallies, tweets, smearing of opponents, "Big Lies," and the "bodily disciplines" of an aggressive, intimidating white alpha masculinity. And, we must add, its often educated women.

If we further add the Foxangelical channeling of the fascistic aspiration, missionary in its spread of the affective contagion, the situation appears troubling indeed. It makes Connolly's answer to the antagonism all the more inviting, and perhaps even realistic. He has long called it an ethos of "agonistic respect."[19] Agonism suggests "struggle" rather than mere enmity. We need not deny that the Trump/Fox amalgam functions as the enemy of an 'us' that seeks race, class, gender, sex, and ecological justice. This is the broad "bandwidth of a democratic, pluralist culture."[20] But while the dramatic threat to that "us" may mobilize more effective national and international coalition, it does not define us. The simple oppositionalism

18. Connolly, *Aspirational Fascism*, 15.

19. See Connolly, *Capitalism and Christianity*, xiv. See also Mouffe, *Return of the Political*. Mouffe describes "agonism" as a third way between liberal consensualism and sheer antagonism, a form of sustained struggle that retains and respects the "vibrant clashes" and "open conflict" upon which any healthy democratic process depends.

20. Connolly, *Aspirational Fascism*, 89.

of antagonism cannot, by definition, be *simply* opposed. It can only be opposed by complexity—and thus complexly, strategically, self-critically.

It is tempting to fantasize that Trumpism will serve to provoke a new revolutionary *us* of resistance. But that fantasy becomes self-destructive, I fear, if it primarily seeks to purify, to reduce to the certainty of the One, our varieties of radicality and motivation. It then trumps the complexity of the actual alliance we now urgently need. The complexity of intersectional pluralism does not brook mere opposition. The fantasy does, however, contain an imaginable truth: Current catastrophe may serve as the catalyst of a rigorously intersectional pluralism. This would be kin to the "multi-faceted pluralism" Connolly seeks for our fragile democracy, and subsequently, for the social democracy it may become.[21]

If radicality translates from a single root into a spreading rhizome, our multiplicity of burning issues—race, class, sexuality, climate, just for starters—ceases to dissipate the political. That pluralism lets the many religions and their secularizations, along with the needed regional variations of tonality and strategy, together fire up the national spectrum of an internationally *ecosocial public*.

If that spectrum is not to remain a specter of its own potential, we arise together not in mere antagonism—to the enemy, let alone to each other. We mind the irritability of our proximate differences. We arise in the agonism of our differences—as struggle not against but *with* each other, toward, yes, an *actually common* good. So common, in fact, that it attracts the needed solidarity of the "undercommons."[22] By way of this positive agonism, through a disciplined resistance to antagonism, through its mindfulness of our own most difficult relations—and yes, through its enemy love—still malleable fringes of the conflicted, passive, or even opposed, public may also be reached. Because of youth or race or gender or class vulnerability, we can effect, here and there, unpredictable, possibly rapidly mounting shifts. Even religious demonstrations—who knows, maybe a WWJD march on the WH?—might find new modes of impact.

Not a chance, if we lose sight of the deep indeterminacy of the world. Our religious, modern, and even leftist, habits have habituated us to dangerous levels of determinism, dumping us into despair when our particular

21. Ibid.
22. Harney and Moten, *Undercommons*.

97

DOING THEOLOGY IN THE AGE OF TRUMP

line of progress fails us. Hence the new activist mantra: "Hope is an embrace of the unknown."[23]

As to "the age of Trump," the vengeful erraticism of the present regime remains perilous. As I write, our political comedians are making us laugh nervously at the presidential boast of "the bigger button," knowing that the Russia investigation may provoke yet more dangerous displays of threatened potency. The very interval between writing this and its publication signifies an alarming degree of unpredictability. But the farcical forty-fifth performs already such high levels of chaotic self-contradiction (very unlike classical fascism) that even its one-term stability is in question.

Importantly for the present argument, such instability infuses the root-shriveling Foxangelical religion as well. That it depends upon the concealment of its own innermost dynamism—a secularist supersession of biblical Christianity—symptomatizes not just its versatile, hyperfunded force but the fragility of self-contradiction. Its overdetermined power does not extract it from its vulnerable indeterminacy. This uncertain level of irreducible indeterminacy may characterize all cosmic happenings.[24] And, for that reason, can make all the difference now.

What has such overdetermined indeterminacy to do with political theology as an option, currently? How does it pertain to the effect of theology on politics—but especially now vice versa? Might we agree, in brief (as I work to finish up also a book-length *Political Theology of the Earth* in response to the present currents), that a constructive, not merely descriptive, political theology must at a certain point surface its own theology? It recognizes in theology a force for secularization in the past—and so also in the present. It reads the secularizations of an all-determining omnipotence—from theocracy to aspirational fascism—as a deep problem for which we in the Christian legacy bear special and confused accountability.[25] So we work to amplify an alternative secularization.

Such an alternative unfolds the history of radical, theologically primed movements, narrated by Ernst Bloch in the three volumes of *The Principle of Hope*: the eventually secularized impetus behind all democratic

23. Solnit, *Hope in the Dark*, xiv.

24. For a vibrantly political reading of this cosmological indeterminacy, see Connolly, *Fragility of Things*, and specifically the chapter called "Process Philosophy and Planetary Politics," 149–78. See also my reading of Connolly on Whitehead, in Keller, *Cloud of the Impossible*, ch. 8, "Crusade, Capital, and Cosmopolis," 239–65.

25. For a preliminary discussion of the problematic of divine power see Keller, *On the Mystery*, ch. 4, "After Omnipotence," 69–90.

and socialist revolutions. It is the alternative to the history of determinist power, though once in power its revolutions often succumbed to antagonistic determinism after all. So it remains a history only sporadically realized, of a prophetic resistance and a messianic collective, as it pulses into the potentiality of the present.[26] That narrative underlies *Apocalypse Now & Then*, helping it to resist its own temptation to a reductive reading of John of Patmos's Revelation to the religion of vengeance it indubitably resources.[27]

As we foster the secularizations of an ecosocial faith, may we at the same time disclose its operative theology? We may find then the yet-evolving contours of a theopoetics lacking from the start in certainty but rich in metaphor. Its God-figuration counters the paternal ghost of omnipotence with an endless, an incomplete, omnipotentiality. It comes darkly, almost illegibly, inscribed as the possibility that does not control but calls.

Calls to what? Well, to an ongoing struggle, prone to creative coalitions and unexpected breakthroughs. Theologically it finds itself sustained, no matter what tragedy, by an unsoppy, cosmically overextended affect. We may call it the *amorous agonism*.[28] It struggles with all that is willing to struggle with it. It opposes all that unifies merely through opposition, and so its agonism respectfully, unyieldingly, repudiates the politics of pure antagonism. In this it does not contradict itself, but it frees itself to honest struggle—avowed uncertainty carried with coalitional confidence.

So it performs an alternative friendship, kin to another Fox, the one who founded the Society of Friends. And it retains the vulnerability of a deep interdeterminacy: it may not finally decide between such primary oppositions as secular and theological; as Christianity and the other Ways; as electoral politics and radical social movements; as national and international, but more, as human and nonhuman planetary systems; and as, of course, politics and religion.

In these latitudes of indeterminacy, such a political theology remains determined to foster the ecosocial good of a planetary public. So it will appear weak before the nationalist power of the right and the global capital of its Foxangelicalism. Often agonizingly weak. But precisely not paralyzed by this vulnerability. For it outgrows the "cruel optimisms," the misdirected

26. See Crockett, *Radical Political Theology*, esp. ch. 8, "Plasticity and the Future of Theology," 145–59.

27. The notion of a counterapocalypse, incorporating elements of the prophetic critique of empire, is here preferred to simple anti-apocalypse. See Keller, *Apocalypse Now and Then*.

28. A key concept in Keller, *Political Theology of the Earth*.

hopes, that blind us to actual possibility.[29] If the political theology of the earth keeps appearing, if "we" keep showing up in multiplying alliances and intersectional coalitions, our weakness reveals a darkly bottomless strength.[30] Able through proximate affection and contagious creativity to renew its world-friendship indefinitely, this agonism appears endless, incomplete, amorously undefeated.

29. Berlant, *Cruel Optimism.*

30. On the subtly creative potency of this dark and bottomless depth, see my writing on "*creatio ex profundis,*" in Keller, *Face of the Deep,* esp. 155–238.

12

White Evangelicals, American Ethnonationalism, and Prospects for Change

DANIEL MILLER

In this essay, I want to advance two significant claims. First, insofar as it now represents the religion of American ethnonationalism, majority-white evangelicalism is a pernicious and dangerous social force.[1] Second, while there is reason to think that this movement will shrink over time, there is no reason to suppose that it will moderate politically in the foreseeable future. Any meaningful counter to evangelicalism as a social force will therefore have to come from the outside.

The claim that American evangelicalism represents a social threat because it has become the de facto religion of American ethnonationalism

1. Defining the term *evangelical* is notoriously difficult, and all definitions have their relative strengths and weaknesses. In the discussion that follows, I define evangelicals primarily in terms of denominational or congregational affiliation. This approach has at least two significant strengths over other approaches (e.g., depending on believers' self-identification as evangelical, on a belief-based definition, and the like). First, such a definition has proven particularly effective in predicting evangelicals' social and political attitudes, which has led to its adoption by a wide range of scholars. Second, this approach effectively reflects the fact that congregational life among theologically conservative Protestants tends to be highly segregated when comparing white conservative Protestants to African American conservative Protestants. While these groups espouse very similar theological beliefs, these shared beliefs have a divergent relation to their respective political attitudes and identification. A denominational/congregational approach makes clear that whiteness is very much a part of what is under discussion here. For the effectiveness of this approach, see Smidt, *American Evangelicals Today*, 54.

builds off of two premises: (1) The contemporary Republican Party has effectively become the party of white American ethnonationalism; (2) identification with the Republican Party has become a constitutive feature of the religious identity of a majority of white American evangelicals.

If the full transformation of the GOP into the party of white American ethnonationalism is not yet a fait accompli, it is rapidly becoming so. This transformation is not a part of the so-called Trump effect; it is not the doing of Donald Trump, and it did not originate in the 2016 U.S. presidential election. On the contrary, Trump is merely a symptom of developments that have been underway within the Republican Party for some time; he is the id of the GOP, bringing into view the dark impulses and drives that have long energized the party at the grassroots level. While even a number of politically conservative commentators have recently acknowledged this basic point,[2] the Republican Party has long been traveling on a trajectory leading to an alt-right-beloved figure such as Trump. The forces represented by Trump have long been evident for those who could spot, who could *feel*, the coded racism of the U.S. war on drugs, of welfare reform, of redistricting, of states' rights defenses of Confederate monuments, of anti-Obama birther theories and rumors of his Islamic faith, of voters simply not being "comfortable" with Obama, of the Tea Party rallies that formed during the Obama years.[3] The list could go on and on. Multiple surveys have confirmed since the election that white anxiety about people of color was a driving force propelling Donald Trump to the presidency.[4] (All of this is to say nothing, of course, of the misogyny and homo- and transphobia within Republican circles as well.)

Trump did not, then, transform the GOP into a party of ethnonationalists. When Trump refuses to straightforwardly denounce white nationalism, when he appoints an attorney general whom the Senate previously failed to confirm as a judge due to concerns of racism, when one of this

---

2. Sykes, *How the Right Lost Its Mind*; Stephens, "Staring at the Conservative Gutter"; Spaeth, Minutes. *New Republic*, 2015; Flake, "My Party Is in Denial"; Gerson, "Conservative Mind Has Become Diseased"; Bardella, "Say Goodbye to Your Republican Party"; Pierce, "Roy Moore"; DeVega, "Donald Trump Has Dropped the GOP's Mask"; Rosenwaltd, "After Charlottesville."

3. See Kendi, *Stamped from the Beginning*; Bonilla-Silva, *Racism without Racists*.

4. Shepard, "Study"; DeVega, "It Was the Racism, Stupid"; DeVega, "Can We Finally Kill off the Zombie Lie?"; McElwee and McDaniel, "Economic Anxiety Didn't Make People Vote for Trump"; Green, "It Was Cultural Anxiety"; May, "Liberals Were Right"; Wood, "Racism Motivated Trump Voters."

attorney general's first significant actions is to scale back Department of
Justice investigations into police shootings of unarmed black men, when
Trump routinely saves his choicest attacks for women of color, when he uses
a racial slur in a meeting with Navajo code-talkers from the Second World
War, and when he retweets extreme right-wing anti-Muslim propaganda
videos, Trump embodies and gives voice to forces that have long circu-
lated within the party he now leads.[5] And in their acceptance of Trump, for
whatever reason (agreement, political cowardice, opportunism), the bulk
of Republicans in government legitimize these same forces. Indeed, this
should not be surprising: They have been willing to draw on these forces
for their own benefit for years, as noted by a number of the conservative
voices previously cited.

So, assertion 1: The GOP is the de facto party of American ethnonationalism. Assertion 2: Majority American evangelicalism represents the
legitimation of this ethnonationalism. Support for Donald Trump among
white evangelicals has been overwhelming. In fact, it has been historic in
its scope: 81 percent of white evangelicals voted for Trump in the 2016
presidential election. This percentage is noteworthy insofar as it is higher
than the percentage of white evangelical votes that Mitt Romney earned in
2012 (78 percent), or that John McCain tallied in 2008 (74 percent), or even
that George W. Bush received in 2004 (78 percent).[6] This support is even
more noteworthy given these evangelicals' self-styled reputation as "values
voters," insofar as Trump seems to embody *none* of the values that have
figured so prominently in that consciousness.

What remains to be developed here is precisely *why* evangelicals supported Trump in such numbers. Explanations for this have not been lacking:
Majority evangelical support for Trump represents the sacrifice of Christian identity for political advantage,[7] shows the influence of the "prosperity
gospel,"[8] suggests an affinity between evangelicalism and authoritarianism,[9]

5. For these respective examples, see Collins, "Trump Repeats Equivocal Charlottesville Rhetoric"; Totenberg, "Jeff Sessions Previously Denied Judgeship"; Williams, "AG
Sessions Says DOJ to 'Pull Back'"; Nelson, "What's Trump's Problem with Black Wom-
en?"; Hafner, "Is 'Pocahontas' a Racial Slur?"; Landers and Masters, "Trump Retweets
Anti-Muslim Videos."

6. Smith and Martinez, "How the Faithful Voted."

7. See Prothero, "Huge Cultural Shift"; Jones, "Donald Trump and the Transformation of White Evangelicals."

8. Posner, "Why Donald Trump's Glitzy Style."

9. Alberts, "American Churches."

came about because leaders have less influence over their flocks,[10] arose because of nostalgia for a lost cultural past,[11] or emerged thanks to a resonance between evangelicalism and American civil religion[12]—and these are just a few explanations. While a number of these proposals offer significant insights, none will support the claim that majority-white evangelicalism has become the de facto religious legitimation of American ethnonationalism. For that, we need a fuller understanding of the relation of majority American evangelicalism to political conservatism.[13]

Explanations for Trump support, such as those surveyed above, typically proceed on the assumption that what requires explanation is why individuals who share a particular religious identity (i.e., white evangelicals) supported a political candidate who does not share that identity or give strong evidence of sharing their values. Such analyses assume, in other words, that in accounting for majority evangelical support for Trump, we are dealing with the conjunction of two discrete social identities—one religious, the other political.

I think this presumption represents a fundamental misunderstanding of the relation of American evangelicals and the GOP. Majority evangelical support for Trump does not result from the convergence of two discrete sociopolitical identities, but is the expression of a *single* religious identity. That is, there is no distinction between a majority of American evangelicals' religious and political identities. Rather, identification as politically conservative is a constitutive feature of the *religious* identity of a majority of white evangelicals in America. The result of this identification is that a vast majority of American evangelicals voted for Trump because they would have supported *any* GOP candidate for president. On an affective, visceral level, it is simply inconceivable to most white evangelicals that one could be a(n) (evangelical) Christian and *not* support the GOP.

Considerations of length are such that I can only outline the main contours of this argument here.[14] The assumption that majority evan-

10. Merritt, "Trump Reveals the End."

11. Jones, "How 'Values Voters.'"

12. Wooley, "Why So Many Evangelicals Support Trump."

13. Considered analytically, political conservatism can obviously be distinguished from the Republican Party; the two are not simply coterminous. In practice, however, there will be very little distinction between them: in the context of contemporary American political life, political conservatism is most likely to manifest itself in support for the Republican Party. In what follows, then, I will us the two terms interchangeably.

14. I make the argument that political conservatism is a constitutive feature of the

gelicalism and political conservatism represent two discrete sociopolitical identities reflects what we can refer to as a "coalitional" understanding of sociopolitical identity. A coalitional identity represents a strategic alliance between two social parties whose discrete identities are preserved within the coalition. On a coalitional model, an examination of widespread evangelical support for Trump seeks the reason why evangelicals have chosen to enter into a strategic alliance with the Republican Party, what their interests are in doing so. It seems clear that in the period of the emergence of the conjunction of evangelicalism and political conservatism from the late 1970s into the early 1980s, we do indeed encounter a coalitional identity. In that context, we find GOP political operatives actively seeking to form a political alliance with evangelicals who had become disillusioned with the Carter administration.[15]

In the current conjunction of majority evangelicalism and support for the GOP, however, we encounter something very different: an equivalential social identity. A relation of equivalence is one in which social groups identify to such an extent that a *new* social identity takes shape, one that cannot be reduced to the identities preexisting its formation.[16] Over time, coalitional sociopolitical identities can evolve into relations of equivalence in which the preexisting identities merge into a single, new social identity and can be differentiated only analytically. This is what has happened in the case of majority evangelicalism and the GOP: The relation between the two has evolved to the point that at present, a majority of evangelicals stand in a relation of equivalence to Republicans and political conservatism so that, understood from the side of majority evangelicalism, they do not represent two discrete social identities. On the contrary, support for the contemporary GOP, in the form of both its party platform and its presidential candidates, is a constitutive dimension of what it means to be an evangelical, as understood by a majority of evangelicals.[17]

---

religious identity of a majority of white American evangelicals in Miller, "Mystery of Evangelical Trump Support?" This article represents the application of the political ontology I develop elsewhere to the question of evangelical support for Trump. See Miller, *Myth of Normative Secularism*, esp. ch. 4, "Political Articulations: The Phenomenology of the Political," 153–97.

    15. See Lambert, *Religion in American Politics*, 196ff.

    16. Miller, *Myth of Normative Secularism*, 186–215.

    17. One piece of evidence for this point is the increasingly conservative positions among white evangelicals on political issues with no clear or explicit "religious" or "moral" tonality, such as the size of government and the federal provision of a social safety net, environmental regulation, and so forth. This increasing degree of political conservatism

If we add to this account of evangelical political identity the role that social identity plays in voting behavior, we gain further clarity regarding overwhelming evangelical support for Trump. As Christopher H. Achen and Larry M. Bartels have convincingly demonstrated, partisan identity is the most significant factor in explaining political behavior.[18] This view, which they dub the "group theory" of democracy, contrasts with the "folk theory" of democracy, according to which partisan identity and voting behavior is an effect of political actors' political ideology, deeply held convictions, and so forth. Political ideology, deep-seated values, issue proximity to elected officials—in short, those aspects of political psychology conventionally understood as determinants of partisan identification—are actually the effects of *prior* partisan identification. As Achen and Bartels put it, when voters do offer reasons for their political actions, they "sound like they're thinking," but "their consistency is often driven by group loyalties and partisan biases, even when it comes to straightforward matters of fact."[19]

If these points are brought together, the logic of evangelical support for Trump comes into clear focus. Given that partisan political identity is a constitutive feature of the religious identity for a majority of American evangelicals, and given the role of political identity in determining political views and behaviors, we should expect precisely what was on clear display in the 2016 presidential election: overwhelming political support for the GOP presidential candidate. Going further, insofar as the Republican Party has become the de facto party of American ethnonationalism, this also means that majority evangelicalism provides the functioning religious legitimation of that ethnonationalism.

It is also important to understand the prereflexive nature of this identification. The deeply affective partisan identities that motivate political action operate on what William Connolly usefully dubs the "visceral register," which he describes as "preconscious modes of intensity and thought-imbued feelings built into the stomach."[20] The political identification of these evangelicals does not reflect a conscious calculation or result from a

is clear when comparing the relative shifts in evangelical positions in 2007 and 2014. See Pew Research Center, *Religious Landscape Study* 2015. While, I am suggesting that identification with the Republican Party and its platform is a constitutive feature of majority evangelicalism, I am not making the corresponding claim that identification with evangelicalism is a constitutive feature of being a Republican. I leave the latter question open.

18. Achen and Bartels, *Democracy for Realists.*

19. Ibid, 296.

20. Connolly, *Why I Am Not a Secularist*, 3, 176.

rational political deliberation; rather, it operates at the "gut-level." As Achen and Bartels suggest, even when political actors bolster their action with "rational-sounding reasons," their real source lies in "emotional or cognitive commitments whose *real basis lies elsewhere.*"[21] Further, this "elsewhere" is likely to be unknown to political actors themselves: "The fact that none of the opinions propping up her party loyalty are really hers will be quite invisible to her. *It will feel like she's thinking.*"[22]

Reason, and the offering of reasons for political support or positions, still plays a role within the group theory of politics, but the role changes radically. While sociopolitical agents can and do offer reasons and rationales for the positions they hold and the political actions they undertake, these are second-order, post facto legitimations of affective identities.[23] When they do elaborate ostensible reasons for their political decisions, then voters "sound like they're thinking," but "their consistency is often driven by group loyalties and partisan biases, even when it comes to straightforward matters of fact."[24] This explains the radical divergence between the rationales offered by evangelicals in support of Trump from those to which evangelicals appealed in their critiques of President Bill Clinton, to give a notable contrasting example. This divergence is difficult to explain at the base of political identity. But if this divergence rests on the effects of a political identity already in effect, then reasons that become after-the-fact rationalizations are just what we should expect.

These considerations bring us back to the central point: Given the GOP's de facto status as the party of white ethnonationalism in America, given that Republican political identity is a constitutive element of the religious identity for a majority of white American evangelicals, and given the significance of group identity to political behavior and beliefs, majority American evangelicalism provides religious legitimation for American

21. Achen and Bartels, *Democracy for Realists*, 268, 269 (italics added).

22. Ibid, 268; italics added. Working from a very different background (evolutionary psychology), Jonathan Haidt makes the same point on psychological and physiological grounds, suggesting that "we find ourselves liking or disliking something the instant we notice it, sometimes even before we know what it is," and notes that not only are these "affective reactions" preconscious or prereflexive, they are even "too fleeting to be called emotions" (Haidt, *Righteous Mind*, 65).

23. Though he does not delve into the subject of identity, Haidt makes essentially the same point, arguing repeatedly that reasoning in issues such as morality is almost always post hoc in nature and is deployed to bolster anterior affective commitments (e.g., ibid., 47, 54).

24. Achen and Bartels, *Democracy for Realists*, 296.

ethnonationalism. For these reasons majority-white evangelicalism in the U.S. represents a pernicious social force that must be actively countered: Countering white ethnonationalism necessarily means working to counter its religious legitimation.

This leads to one final area of consideration: Such a pernicious expression of evangelicalism will not be effectively countered from within. Those who believe that it will commonly identify at least two potential forces of change. The first is a certain "evangelical left" represented by figures such as Ronald Sider, Tony Campolo, and Jim Wallis; the expressed hope is that these theologically conservative but socially moderate or progressive leaders represent some sort of evangelical counteroffensive. I think any such faith is misplaced. For one, the organizations of this "evangelical left" tend to center on "a magnetic and captivating personality" and therefore face difficulties maintaining their identity and social momentum as their charismatic founders age and retire.[25] For another, in many cases, these movements do not clearly represent evangelicalism to begin with. Wallis serves as a prime illustration: While evangelical subscriptions to *Sojourners* (Wallis's flagship publication) increased from 5 percent of readership in 2002 to 18 percent in 2011, evangelicals still represent a significant minority, with the effect that the publication still resides on the fringes of evangelicalism.[26] It is, then, not surprising that the overall effect of this "evangelical left" has been relatively insignificant.[27]

The second commonly identified source of salvation-from-within are millennial evangelicals. A lot of ink has been spilled (or pixels arranged) arguing that millennial evangelicals represent a force for change in the future of evangelicalism.[28] And, on the face of it, this might be a compelling argument, insofar as a lot of evidence exists that millennial evangelicals swing further to the left than their generationally older brethren, and that

25. Black, "Evangelicals," 143.

26. Ibid., 144. Black also notes that 15 percent of the readership identify with the "emerging church" movement, a group that includes some evangelicals. This is almost certainly correct, though determining the portion of this group that could be identified as evangelical would be difficult. In its classification of Protestant religious traditions, the Pew Research Center lists the "Emergent Church" as a nondenominational mainline Protestant tradition.

27. See ibid., 145.

28. Pally, *New Evangelicals*; Rah, *Next Evangelicalism*;and Lee, *Rescuing Jesus*; Webber, *Younger Evangelicals*; Lee, "Why the Young"; Rubin, "Younger Evangelicals."

they don't differ markedly in their social views from millennials in other Christian traditions.[29]

But, again, this faith is misplaced, for two reasons. The first is that there simply aren't enough millennial evangelicals to make a significant impact on the larger body of evangelicalism. Millennials are an underrepresented group among evangelicals, and there's reason to think that evangelicalism is failing to retain the millennials currently within the movement (which is partially responsible for evangelicalism's declining numbers).[30] The second reason involves greater prognostication, but I believe it is still well-founded: Most socially moderate or progressive evangelicals will *leave* evangelicalism rather than transforming it. By far, the religiously unaffiliated (so-called nones) is the group with which millennials are most likely to identify,[31] and, significantly, a large proportion of nones reject organized religion *because of* its perceived identification with political conservatism.[32] If we combine these insights with the recognition that a sizable number of evangelicals actually *did* leave their congregations in direct response to the 2016 presidential election,[33] I think this trend line is clear.[34]

In summary, I believe that it is increasingly difficult for those who do not identify with the GOP to remain within evangelicalism, with the result that they do, or will, leave; the social, emotional, and spiritual costs of attempting to reform the movement will simply be too high. Looking to the future, we can expect accounts of evangelical "leavers" to become more numerous and prominent.[35] David P. Gushee's account is particularly telling in this regard, insofar as it gives voice to many of the trajectories more clinically or analytically on display here. Most notably, Gushee, whose academic achievements and evangelical credentials are significant, notes on

29. Smidt, *American Evangelicals Today*, 205–8.

30. Cox and Jones, "America's Changing Religious Identity"; Pew Research Center, *Religious Landscape Study*, "Evangelical Protestants." Putnam and Campbell, *American Grace*, 131; Pew Research Center, "Faith in Flux"; Lipka, "Millennials."

31. Pew Research Center, *Religious Landscape Study*, "Generational Cohort"; Cox and Jones, "America's Changing Religious Identity."

32. Zuckerman, *Living the Secular Life*, 67; Mercadante, *Belief without Borders*, 27; Nicolaou, *None's Story*, xi; Hout and Fischer, "Why More Americans"; Putnam and Campbell, *American Grace*.

33. Djupe et al., "How Fights over Trump."

34. Wallis, "White American Evangelical."

35. For two such accounts, see Evans, *Searching for Sunday*; and Gushee, *Still Christian*.

more than one occasion that a significant factor in his movement out of evangelicalism was the equivalence of majority-white evangelicalism with the Republican Party. He captures this point by defining the present era as one in which "*GOP=(white) evangelical* in the same way that *search=Google* and *lip balm=ChapStick*."[36] Decrying the significance of this equivalence within his own context of the evangelical academy, he writes,

> Christian college faculty sign doctrinal statements filled with all kinds of theological claims to which they promise adherence. They do not sign political loyalty oaths. But I am not the only one to discover that those political loyalties are often the subtext of white evangelical higher education. You discover that when you violate them in a manner visible enough to attract serious attention.[37]

David Gushee and Rachel Held Evans are unique only in being in positions to give such articulate voice to their experiences of evangelical alienation. There are thousands of disillusioned evangelicals, particularly younger evangelicals, for every Evans and Gushee, and every indication is that they will confront only two realistic options: accommodate themselves to the increasingly conservative political ideology of majority-white evangelicalism, or leave.

To expect large-scale political moderation of majority-white American evangelicalism is not therefore realistic. Looking to the future of evangelicalism, a more realistic prediction is that the movement will shrink as an overall percentage of the US population but will remain overwhelming homogeneous and increasingly conservative politically. Any effective efforts to counter this social movement will have to come from outside its ranks.

36. Gushee, *Still Christian*, 124 (italics original).
37. Ibid., 101.

13

Trumpism Is a State of Affairs

JORDAN E. MILLER AND HOLLIS PHELPS

It is relatively simple to point to belief systems and practices of people who support Trump and his presidency. We are not sold that's the most effective or useful way of understanding Trumpism, though. Rather than a set of political, social, or theological positions, we argue Trumpism is a condition in which we all find ourselves. We are living in the age of Trumpism. Trumpism is the name of an accelerating series of political, social, and environmental crises buttressed by a nihilistic capitalism. Trumpism is not a belief. It's a state of affairs.

It will be helpful to focus in on a short period of time recently to see how Trumpism operates. During the week of September 10–16, 2017:

The United Nations Security Council had just voted to impose new sanctions on North Korea about a week after its sixth and largest-to-date nuclear weapons test.[1] "Although the new sanctions are the harshest yet, they could have been a lot tougher. A full oil import ban and sanctions on Kim Jong Un himself were dropped at the last minute, in a possible attempt by the U.S. to gain the support of Russia and China." North Korea responded a few days later by launching a ballistic missile over northern Japan. "The South carried out a 'live fire drill' and launched a missile it says could reach Pyongyang."[2]

---

1. Cohen and Roth, "UN Passes Fresh Sanctions."
2. Criss, "5 Things for September 15."

Meanwhile, in Phoenix Arizona, Motel 6 employees went on the record that "We send a report every morning to ICE [Immigration and Customs Enforcement]—all the names of everybody that comes in. Every morning at about 5 o'clock, we do the audit and we push a button and it sends it to ICE."[3] At least twenty people staying at one of two Phoenix Motel 6 locations have been arrested so far in 2017 and sent to immigration detention centers. This was only possible because *every single person* staying in the motel was being reported to ICE and checked against Department of Homeland Security databases for records of illegal entry to the country or prior deportations.[4]

After Hurricane Irma caused severe damage in the U.S. Virgin Islands, governor Kenneth Mapp reached out to the State of New York for help, given its close historical ties to the Caribbean. One hundred members of the New York Army National Guard's 105th Military Police Company and thirty New York State Police officers were sent to help to prevent looting in St. Thomas and St. John.[5]

> The team will bring 12 Humvees and six all-terrain gator utility vehicles to augment security on the island . . . The team will deploy from Niagara Falls Air Reserve Station on board three C-17 Globemaster III cargo aircraft. Members of the 105th Military Police Company deployed to Iraq in 2004 and 2011 and deployed to Guantanamo Bay in 2015.[6]

Returning from a trip to Florida to survey the damage from Hurricane Irma, Trump doubled down on his comments that antifascist protestors, or Antifa, were equally to blame for violence that unfolded at the white supremacist rally in Charlottesville, Virginia, on August 12.[7] Meanwhile,

> State and federal environmental regulators have issued a blanket waiver for Florida electricity companies to violate clean air and water standards for the next two weeks. The Environmental Protection Agency announced the decision in a letter issued Monday as Hurricane Irma blew through the state. The agency said the so-called No Action Assurance granted through Sept. 26 will provide

3. Farzan and Flaherty, "Attorneys Suspect."
4. Farzan, "Motel 6 Locations" (interview by Ari Shapiro).
5. Tacopino, "Cuomo Deploys National Guard."
6. Office of Governor Andrew Cuomo, "Governor Cuomo Deploys National Guard."
7. Criss, "5 Things for September 15."

Florida utility generators needed flexibility to maintain and restore electricity supplies.

The assurance letter will allow utilities to operate outside restrictions mandated by their permits, including potentially using dirtier fuels, running for longer hours or electively bypassing pollution-control equipment. The Associated Press reported last week that air pollution levels spiked in the Houston area after a similar enforcement waiver was granted to petrochemical facilities ahead of Hurricane Harvey.[8]

The situation in North Korea was escalating. Private citizens working for private companies were reporting everyone's information to whom they had access to be checked against Homeland Security databases. Hurricane Irma had destroyed the U.S. Virgin Islands, leaving people starving and desperate, so the governor responded by calling in militarized police to protect private property there. The president argued that antifascists were equally to blame for white supremacist violence. And to accelerate the return to business as usual after disaster, environmental regulators in Florida scrapped environmental protections. When the closing bell on Wall Street rang on Friday, September 16, the Dow was up 2 percent for the week, hitting all-time high after a sixth straight day of gains. The S&P 500 and the Nasdaq both hit new records as well.[9]

That the market would continue to rise, without so much as a hiccup—and has risen consistently throughout Trump's presidency, clocking in at record highs—evinces the way the market capitalizes on disaster.[10] Crises don't impede the market but rather accelerate it, as the few profit from the misfortune of the many. Appeals to charity in such circumstance and promises to rebuild conceal the way such disasters are "good" for the economy in the long run, at least for those who control its "invisible hand." Moreover, naturalizing such disasters (i.e. it's a hurricane and thus out of our control) ignores the ways political, social, and economic decisions create the threats we face, or at least exacerbate them. The market, in this sense, fabricates at a structural level the very disasters on which it will capitalize; in religious terms, this is similar to the way God floods the earth in the story of Noah (Gen 6–8) in order to extract obedience and faith.

8. CBS/Associated Press, "Irma Leaves Widespread Devastation, Flooding in Florida—live updates," CBSNews.com, September 12, 2017, https://www.cbsnews.com/news/irma-live-updates-florida-power-outages-09–11–2017.

9. Monica, "No Worries on Wall Street."

10. See Klein, *Shock Doctrine.*

Nevertheless, capitalizing on disaster—indeed, we could say on the Disaster that is Trumpism—isn't a market anomaly, some abuse of the system that could be remedied through mere reform. Profiting from disaster is, rather, part and parcel of a financialized economy that relates to material conditions via abstraction. Otherwise put, what matters is not so much material conditions in and of themselves but rather the way these conditions can be packaged to generate capital so that the financial economy can operate at continuing levels of remove from conditions on the ground (so to speak), in and for itself. Although we might be tempted to suggest that the disconnect, here, resides in the distinction of the abstract, financial economy from the so-called real economy, we should resist conceptualizing the problem in that way. The financial economy is, rather, the "real" economy, which means that we are always already caught in the mandates of the former,[11] which also means that we are always already treated as abstractions—or as disasters waiting to happen.

This is one way we can understand that horribly poignant video of Trump throwing paper towels into the crowd of displaced and disaster-weary Puerto Ricans. The act was, of course, insensitive: it suggested that the situation was a carnival, and did not truly meet the material needs of the island's inhabitants. Trump seems a particularly insensitive person, aloof from the realities of most people, especially those in crisis. Nevertheless, we should not read the way Trump handled the situation in individualistic terms only. His act brings to the surface in a condensed, public fashion our state of affairs.

Responses to all this tend to fall into one of two camps: defensive support or abhorrence. These two responses are prompted by the spectacle of the disaster presidency. When faced with this kind of crisis, a choice is prompted to either accept or reject the spectacle (hence the common injunctions to either unite or resist). But both of these postures rely on a kind of personal piety and a superstition in order to operate. They play the same game, mirroring each other; this is seen, for instance, in the constant back-and-forth lobbing of pithy, ineffectual memes on social media.

This either/or, for/against reaction to Trump's presidency manifests itself in numerous ways. One way it arises is in the charge of hypocrisy against Trump and Trump's supporters. We see this especially in criticism of white evangelical support for Trump, where such criticism attempts to point out the apparent disconnect between so-called evangelical values and

11. See Marazzi, *Violence of Financial Capitalism*.

political fealty. The problem with hypocrisy as a charge is that it assumes that statements take the form of good faith; it is assumed in advance that statements correspond with material actions. One is a hypocrite, that is, to the extent that what one does, in word or act, conflicts with one's stated belief. Criticism of a putatively hypocritical position, then, calls out the offending party in the hope that exposing the disconnect between belief and action will resolve the apparent contradiction, aligning the two once again in a coherent position. The accusation of hypocrisy is an attack upon one's personal moral purity. It's an assault on another's piety and follows the same logic of superstition. Such a stance, however, fails to account for the way ideas manifest themselves within specific discourses, which may have their own rules. Although from the outside evangelical support for Trump may appear contradictory and hypocritical, within the evangelical imaginary it is not necessarily. In actual discourse and practice, that support makes sense, and has narrative support, even if we may ultimately recoil at such support for whatever reason. Moreover, the hypocrisy charge fails to account for the fact that individuals do not normally consider themselves as hypocritical.

That's, in part, the whole point of critique: to bring to light what was previously concealed. Nevertheless, this goal assumes a universal standard outside the functioning of discourse. What looks contradictory or hypocritical from the outside may not be so from within a particular discourse. Likewise, it ignores the role of affect in the positions we take. What we believe is not merely an intellectual affair, a cognitive attachment to certain positions and overall discourses. What we believe is, rather, felt, located in our bodies—and that goes for religion and politics. As Spinoza has written, "Superstition . . . is sustained only by hope, hatred, anger, and deceit. For it arises not from reason but from emotion, and emotion of the most powerful kind."[12] Unfortunately, it appears that Trump understands this better than his opponents, at least among those who loosely identify themselves as liberals. Whether we like it or not, arguments against Trump won't work, because that's not how politics works, not how religion works. It's not how Trumpism works.

Another reaction against Trump's presidency is the common injunction to "resist." The sites of resistance proposed are invariably personal. To combat Trump's assault on the Environmental Protection Agency, make sure you turn the lights off when you leave a room. To oppose the travel

12. Spinoza, *Theological-Political Treatise*, 2.

ban against Muslims, call your congressperson to register your opinion. Lament and ridicule the tweet. Wear a pink hat.

The largest organized group with the mandate to resist Trump is the Indivisible movement. It self-consciously has adopted tactics and strategies developed by the Tea Party to resist Obama's presidency. As Indivisible writes,

> The authors of this guide are former congressional staffers who witnessed the rise of the Tea Party. We saw these activists take on a popular president with a mandate for change and a supermajority in Congress. We saw them organize locally and convince their own MoCs [members of Congress] to reject President Obama's agenda. Their ideas were wrong, cruel, and tinged with racism—and they won. We believe that protecting our values, our neighbors, and ourselves will require mounting a similar resistance to the Trump agenda—but a resistance built on the values of inclusion, tolerance, and fairness.[13]

"Resistance" has become the piety and the superstition of the anti-Trumper. It is a sacred notion. But it is cheaply bought. As Dietrich Bonhoeffer once wrote of Christendom's cheap grace—a grace "sold on the market like cheapjacks' wares," a grace without any existential risk[14]—anti-Trumpers practice a cheap resistance. It is resistance without risk—without faith—for it refuses to question its own conditions. It is a resistance that only responds and makes no claims to a new world that we might build.

Our task is to play a different game entirely. But what would a different game look like? Based on what we have said, it can't take the form of simple opposition to Trump, or even principled resistance. A Bartleby-style politics of "preferring not to" won't cut it, because Trumpism doesn't name a person or a belief but a state of affairs—a state in which we always already find ourselves, whether we like it or not. Otherwise put, much of the opposition to Trump assumes that the current state of affairs is a given; politics, in this sense, takes the form of signaling our disgust—our piety—and is, ultimately, reduced to electing "better" managers of the situation in which we find ourselves.

We must, rather, change the state of affairs itself, and this involves theological critique and construction. Theological, because the stakes are theological in the sense that the current realities we must confront concern,

---

13. Indivisible, "Introduction to the Guide."

14. Bonhoeffer, *Cost of Discipleship*, 45–47.

as Tillich might say, the ground of our existence or being. That ground, we must note, is not located in an Other, in what we commonly name as God, but is, rather, found in the material conditions of existence itself. Tillich reminds us that, "the risk of faith is an existential risk, a risk in which the meaning and fulfillment of our lives is at stake, and not a theoretical judgment which may be refuted sooner or later."[15] So this is the theological task during Trumpism: we must change our state of affairs through the transformation of the material conditions of our existence.

15. Tillich, *Theology of Culture*, 20.

14

Donald Trump, Republican Beloved

JOE BESSLER

It's time to wake up . . . We have to fight against propaganda and crack-pot conspiracy theories. We have to fight isolationism, protectionism and nativism. We have to defeat those who would worsen our divisions. We have to remind our sons and daughters that we became the most power-ful nation on earth by tearing down walls, not building them.[1]
—REPUBLICAN SENATOR JOHN MCCAIN

It must also be said that I rise today with no small measure of regret. Regret because of the state of our disunion. Regret because of the disrepair and destructiveness of our politics. Regret because of the indecency of our discourse. Regret because of the coarseness of our leadership. Regret for . . . all of our complicity in this alarming and dangerous state of affairs. It is time for our complicity and our accommodation of the unacceptable to end.[2]
—REPUBLICAN SENATOR JEFF FLAKE

"I don't know why the President tweets out things that are not true. You know he does it, everyone knows he does it, but he does."[3]
—REPUBLICAN SENATOR ROBERT CORKER

1. See Meixler, "'It's Time to Wake Up'" (includes full transcript of McCain's address).
2. *The Hill*, "Transcript: Flake Announces Retirement."
3. Cillizza, "12 Most Damning Bob Corker Quotes."

Leaving the Yard

I found myself listening to the above remarks from senior Republican senators in October of 2017 while leading several class sessions on Toni Morrison's novel *Beloved*. As I took in these comments my mind went to the figure of Denver, who, late in the novel, realizes that the haunting figure of Beloved is draining the life from her mother, Sethe. The threat of Beloved's presence had become visible to Denver only gradually. While she had once, out of her own loneliness, doted on Beloved, Denver now sees that the figure of Beloved threatens not only Sethe's life but also the quality of her own. "Somebody," she realizes, "had to be saved."[4] And her conviction that Beloved is haunting, possessing, her mother forces on Denver another truth: namely, as sociologist Avery Gordon says, "the necessity of doing something about it."[5]

In order to get help for her mother, to get herself a job, Denver knows she will need to go outside a gate and cross a threshold she had not traversed for a long time for fear of the violence and rejection she would experience beyond it. She will have to leave the space of her yard. She "stood on the porch in the sun and couldn't leave it." She stood frozen in place until she heard the voice of her dead grandmother, Baby Suggs:

> [Denver's] throat itched; her heart kicked—and then Baby Suggs laughed, clear as anything. "You mean I never told you nothing about Carolina? About your daddy? You don't remember nothing about how come I walk the way I do and about your mother's feet, not to speak of her back? I never told you all that? Is that why you can't walk down the steps? My Jesus my."
> But you said there was no defense.
> "There ain't."
> Then what do I do?
> "Know it, and go on out the yard. Go on."[6]

While I feel the strangeness of setting the character of Denver and the story of *Beloved* alongside the words of powerful, white, Republican, male senators, I do so because I see both sets of characters attempting to find courageous footing in a haunted world. And so, Denver's awakening to her own

---

4. Morrison, *Beloved*, 252.

5. Gordon, *Ghostly Matters*, 206.

6. Morrison, *Beloved*, 244.

responsibility in confronting what is haunting her mother and family is itself a transformative moment.

Writing about the phenomenon of being haunted, Gordon in her work *Ghostly Matters: Haunting and the Sociological Imagination* says that such experience "draws us affectively, sometimes against our will, and always a bit magically, into the structure of a reality we come to experience, not as cold knowledge, but as transformative recognition."[7] The discomfort McCain, Flake, and Corker feel is palpable as they struggle to come to grips with the social forces that a president of their own party has courted and let loose in the country. Like Denver, I think they see and feel at a visceral level what is at stake in allowing those social forces—white supremacist violence in Charlottesville, Virginia; the Alabama senatorial campaign of Roy Moore; the constant, daily attempts of a Trump White House to undermine the integrity of the press, the findings of science, the leadership of women in public life—to metastasize into a discourse of narcissistic fascism.

Beyond the necessity of leaving the yard, Denver also knows she would have to tell the story of her mother, of Beloved, of their lives at 124 Bluestone Road. "Nobody was going to help her unless she told it—told all of it."[8] It is that act of taking responsibility and confession, as it were, that begins to weaken the hold and the power of possession. To be sure, it is not clear whether these three senators, or others moved by them, will have the courage to tell "all of it," to name the party's deep complicity over the past fifty years in stoking a culture of white resentment that longs for a lost order of racial and male hegemony.[9]

Haunting and Its Challenge

In December of 2015, commenting on the surprise of Trump's victories in the Republican primaries, I wrote an article in which I sought to make evident the conundrum of the Republican Party in dealing with the candidacy of Donald Trump.

---

7. Gordon, *Ghostly Matters*, 8.

8. Morrison, *Beloved*, 253.

9. Williams, *White Working Class*. While Democrats and liberals have their own hand in failing to attend adequately to both working-class dignity and working-class jobs for whites as well as blacks and all persons of color, Republicans have systematically stoked the rhetoric of racial, gender, class, and white religious resentment.

A recent Tom Toles political cartoon captures the dilemma well. Two elephants are talking with one another. The first says, "We've got a Trump problem." To which the other responds, "He's appealing to voters who are responding to racism bordering on fascism." The first says, "It's a real dilemma," with the other asking a concluding question, "How do we get rid of Trump but keep those voters?"

As the cartoon brilliantly illustrates, what Republicans have yet to own, but cannot do so publicly, is that Donald Trump is not the real problem. The real problem is the audience they have created and catered to during the last 50 years.[10]

From the time of Nixon's 1968 Southern Strategy, but especially since Ronald Reagan's explicit call in his February 6, 1977, speech titled, "The New Republican Party," to bring "fiscal conservatives" and "social conservatives" together, Republican campaigns have winked at, tacitly encouraged, and rhetorically played to resentments that the Civil Rights Act of 1964 and the Voting Rights Act of 1965 had sought to put to rest. Republicans have not sought over the past fifty years to "bind up the wounds of the nation," as their founder, Lincoln, encouraged in his second inaugural address. Instead, the party's electoral strategy has been to pour salt on those wounds.

The strategy has been a metonymic one, invoking the violation of *boundaries*—sacred, natural, and constitutional—to create a culture of suspicion and fear in need of defense, of protection, of guns. There was Reagan, on August 3, 1980, at the Neshoba County Fair in Mississippi, opening his national campaign with a speech proclaiming, "I believe in states' rights."[11] Throughout that campaign, Reagan would link his voice to Jerry Falwell's Moral Majority and to Phyllis Schlafly's fear of feminists—all appealing to traditional or sacred boundaries that had been crossed and defiled. Over the years the appeals to a now-lost old order were sounded in virtually each election cycle. Some of those appeals include "teaching the controversy" between evolution and creationism, placing initiatives on state ballots against gay marriage to turn out the vote, adding every imaginable impediment to keep black and poor people from voting, making it increasingly difficult for women to have access to reproductive health care or to receive care in

10. Bessler, "In Trump."

11. *Neshoba Democrat*, Transcript of Ronald Reagan's 1980 Neshoba County Fair Speech.

ending unwanted or unhealthy pregnancies, and ignoring the science of climate change while promising to reinvigorate the coal industry.[12]

In 2015–16, there had been signs that the Republican Party—out of its own need to be competitive nationally—seemed intent on moving away from its established pattern. In figures such as the presumed favorite Jeb Bush, the younger Marco Rubio, the African American Ben Carson, and even in Republican moderates such as John Kasich, who had accepted the Affordable Care Act in Ohio, the party seemed to recognize the need to reach out to women, to Hispanics, to African Americans—to become a party of greater inclusion. Into that mix entered the rude, crude, belittling, Twittering figure of Donald Trump, whose ugly rhetoric signaled his disdain for those proposed shifts in Republican culture. The eerily haunting character of his "I am your voice" rhetoric at the Republican National Convention,[13] was onomatopoetic of the frustrations that CNN commentator Van Jones called, on election night, a "whitelash against a changing country."[14]

The unexpectedness of Trump's victory and what it revealed of America's political, racial, and religious divide matches Gordon's analysis: "The ghostly haunt says, Something is happening you hadn't expected. It says, Something is making an appearance to you that had been kept from view. It says, Do something about the wavering present the haunting is creating."[15] In truth, Trump is not Other. He is not an outlier to the Republican brand, as many Republicans have tried to claim; he's the backward-looking, making-America-great-again, white, male savior Republicans have been promising for fifty years. That Trump played to those resentments so successfully, and did so *against* the Republican Party establishment, has made glaringly apparent the moral ugliness of the political game that Republicans have been playing for decades. In his closing remarks on his MSNBC program *Hardball* on October 26, 2017, Chris Matthews called the transformation of Republicans into the image of Trump, an "Invasion of the Body Snatchers." Members of the Republican Party, he said, are becoming "Trumpites," "no longer the actual people we thought we knew."[16] There is something

12. Douglas, *Stand Your Ground*. Douglas offers an important critique of the ideology of "stand your ground" gun legislation.

13. *Politico*, "Full Text."

14. See Jones's comments here: https://www.youtube.com/watch?v=MA9aSvHzEIU.

15. Gordon, *Ghostly Matters*, 178–79.

16 MSNBC, "Defense Secretary Mattis."

"magical," something uncanny, that Gordon mentioned: the bizarre and profoundly disturbing possession of the party by the ghosts of its rhetorical past. And yet, as Gordon suggests, the ghost is not simply a past reality but a "living" one: "the ghost figures what systematically continues to work on the here and now."[17]

Morrison, "Mourning for Whiteness"

Following the presidential election in 2016, Toni Morrison joined fifteen other writers in commenting on Trump's election for the *New Yorker*. In her brief essay, "Mourning for Whiteness," Morrison argues that Trump was elected because of his appeal to the fear in white people over the loss of their status in a post–civil rights world: "So scary are the consequences of a collapse of white privilege that many Americans have flocked to a political platform that supports and translates violence against the defenseless as strength. These people are not so much angry as terrified, with the kind of terror that makes knees tremble."[18] As in her novel where the ghost, Beloved, is itself rooted in sadness and profound mourning, Morrison *here*—in her postelection essay—locates the source of white rage in the fear and terror of lost cultural power, its ensuing shame, and its turn to violence.

She notes that "so many white voters—both the poorly educated and the well-educated—embraced the shame and fear sowed by Donald Trump." But beyond that, she suggests that it is the fear and anxiety for a lost order that drives some to acts of incredible violence.

> In order to . . . restore whiteness to its former status as a marker of national identity, a number of white Americans are sacrificing themselves. They have begun *to do things they clearly don't really want to be doing*, and, to do so, they are (1) abandoning their sense of human dignity and (2) risking the appearance of cowardice. Much as they may hate their behavior, and know full well how craven it is, they are willing to kill small children attending Sunday school and slaughter churchgoers who invite a white boy to pray.[19]

The words Morrison italicizes in this passage—that these people 'have begun *to do things they clearly don't really want to be doing*,' alludes to lines

17. Gordon, *Ghostly Matters*, 179.
18. Morrison, "Mourning for Whiteness."
19. Ibid.; italics original.

from a stunning passage in *Beloved*. Late in the novel, one of her characters, Stamp Paid, notes that the subhuman, violent "jungle" that white people assumed to be present within each and every black person—a jungle that "whitepeople put there"—was, in fact, also present in whites. The passage deserves quoting at length:

> Whitepeople believed that whatever the manners, under every dark skin was a jungle. Swift unnavigable waters, swinging scream-ing baboons, sleeping snakes, red gums ready for their sweet white blood . . . The more coloredpeople spent their strength trying to convince them [whites] how gentle they were, how clever and lov-ing, how human, the more they used themselves up to persuade whites of something Negroes believed could not be questioned, the deeper and more tangled the jungle grew inside them. But it wasn't the jungle blacks brought with them to this place from the other (livable) place. It was the jungle whitefolks planted in them. And it grew. It spread. In, through and after life, it spread, until it invaded the whites who had made it. Touched them every one. *Changed and altered them. Made them bloody, silly, worse than even they wanted to be, so scared were they of the jungle they had made.* The screaming baboon lived under their own white skin; the red gums were their own.[20]

In my own reading of Morrison's novel I find it is that jungle that haunts the minds and hearts in our public life and political culture. That Morrison's postelection essay alludes to this passage in *Beloved* is not by chance. Her image in the essay of whites "sacrificing themselves" suggests the linkage of white supremacy to Christian theism. There is good reason to make that connection: the God of European colonialism and racist slav-ery is a white God—a God who dwells quite literally in inapproachable light. When one sees the staggering percentage of white, male Christian evangelicals (upwards of 80 percent) who voted for Donald Trump,[21] one understands the dismay in Morrison's essay:

> On Election Day, how eagerly so many white voters—both the poorly educated and the well educated—embraced the shame and fear sowed by Donald Trump. The candidate whose company has been sued by the Justice Department for not renting apartments to black people. The candidate who questioned whether Barack Obama was born in the United States, and who seemed to condone

20. Morrison, *Beloved*, 198–99 (italics added).
21. Smith and Martinez, "How the Faithful Voted."

the beating of a Black Lives Matter protester at a campaign rally. The candidate who kept black workers off the floors of his casinos. The candidate who is beloved by David Duke and endorsed by the Ku Klux Klan.[22]

"Something-to-be-done"[23]

"Haunting," says, Gordon, "is a frightening experience."[24] Its strangeness can bewilder, isolate, and silence those it comes to possess. That is why Gordon also writes that haunting, "unlike trauma, is distinctive for producing a something-to-be-done."[25] The Westar Institute was organized against a backdrop of resurgent, politicized fundamentalism of the late 1970s and early 1980s. In their introduction to *The Five Gospels*, Bob Funk and Roy Hoover called on scholars to engage in a process of public visibility:

> Academic folk are a retiring lot. We prefer books to lectures, and solitude to public display. Nevertheless, we have too long buried our considered views of Jesus and the gospels in technical jargon and in obscure journals. We have hesitated to contradict TV evangelists and pulp religious authors for fear of political reprisal and public controversy. And we have been intimidated by promotion and tenure committees to whom the charge of popularizing or sensationalizing biblical issues is anathema. It is time for us to quit the library and speak up.[26]

In the language of *Beloved* that I have been using here, Funk and Hoover were saying to biblical scholars, it is time "to leave the yard"—time to leave the security of the library or the sacredness of the divinity school—to risk speech in the public realm. In their play of "buried" voices and "speak[ing] up," one hears the language of resurrection in a new, more urgent, political key. What they said then needs to be said now. Whether in their language of "speaking up" or McCain's language of "waking up," political and theological voices need to move beyond—in Gordon's words—"a dull curiosity or detached know-it-all criticism into *the passion of what is at stake*."[27]

22. Morrison, "Mourning for Whiteness."
23. Gordon, *Ghostly Matters*, xvi.
24. Ibid.
25. Ibid.
26. Funk et al., *Five Gospels*, 34.
27. Gordon, *Ghostly Matters*, 203 (italics added).

Funk's call for scholars "to quit the library," echoes Denver's realization that it is time to leave the yard. For the God Seminar and progressive theologians more generally, exploring the *event* of Donald Trump's candidacy and election will involve exposing the ways that variations of Christian God language that were operative in that event have encouraged gross ignorance of science; dismissal of evidence-based news reporting; and disrespect for women, GBLTQ persons, and for people of color. This public work may take the form of God Seminars on the Road addressing the interrelated themes of race, gender, and Christian nationalism, or the form of our own stories—as a group of largely white, male scholars—about how the inheritance of racist and sexist traditions has been at work in us, subtly shaping our own patterns of avoidance that have kept us safe within the practice of the guild and within the comfort of our own yards. If the work is to be transformative culturally, it will have to be so personally. But to be personally transforming, we will have to leave the yard.

15

Taking Advantage

Trumpism, Postmodernity, and Christianity

DAVID GALSTON

Fundamentalist Christian nationalism, which I will refer to generically as the Christian Right, is either rising or falling in the United States of America. It's hard to tell, but the election of Donald Trump as president appears to summon a victory for the religious Right and its hitherto unsuccessful agenda of "Christian values." These values, in the Trump administration, have so far been restricted to ensuring that it is safe to say merry Christmas—something most Americans worry little about.[1] Other so-called Christian values on the Right consist of antichoice legislation, anti-immigration legislation, anti–health care legislation, and antiscience legislation. We might note two things in relation to this larger agenda. First, very little of it has been successfully established despite the years of courtship and marriage between the Republican Party and the Christian Right. Second, the values in question are not Christian values in any case. The Christian Right sold its soul to the Republican Party sometime in the 1980s, at which point it ceased to hold the integrity of the Christian faith. The Christian

---

1. While the vast majority of Americans love to celebrate Christmas, Pew research shows that most do not really care what greeting or image one chooses to use. The Pew study is referenced in the December 14, 2017, edition of the *New York Times*.

Right is now politics, and what should really concern Americans is the loss of the separation of church and state.

It is right to express concern over the rise of Christian nationalism touted so strongly by the Right, but it is equally correct to see this trend as being more like a return to the distant past rather than an aberration from historical norms. Only during the first three centuries of its rise and the recent three centuries after the Enlightenment has Christianity been relatively free from the obligations of nationalism and state ideologies. Rather, through most of its history in the West, Christianity has been nationalism by another name. Indeed, the Christian and Jewish Bible is filled with nationalism as the expressed face of God. Nationalism and its troubles for the human family are the fallout of the belief that God chooses a state or a church and is therefore restricted in identity to the defense of such institutions. Nationalism makes God both extremely small and extremely confined, which makes nationalism a type of anti-God.

The modern political practice was to free Christianity from nationalism and state ideologies with the separation of religion from the state, thus liberating God from nationalism's prison and resting the national good on the rights of the citizen regardless of religious practice or lack of practice. Yet, one of the unintended side effects of this otherwise noble act has surfaced in the postmodern critique of modernity and the contemporary Christian Right's attempt to use this critique to reauthorize in modern guise lingering medieval notions of religion, hierarchy, and the nation. The expressed side effect of postmodernity consists of religious practices and ideas assuming equivalent authority to modern science and technology and, therefore, justifying medieval-like understandings of nation, class, economic privilege, gender identity, and religious primacy as authoritative truth.

Permission for this reauthorization of modern authority within postmodern culture rests on a twofold foundation. First, postmodern cultural pluralism is taken advantage of to pose any idea as equivalent to any other idea, whether valid or not. Postmodernity suggests that the first one to act and to state a reality is also the first one to set the agenda for reality. When President Trump tweets something, however ridiculous, it becomes the news and the subject of debate. It sadly becomes equivalent to important, socially relevant, and meaningful issues in the life of the state. Bravado over the president's intelligence or lack thereof is entirely abstract from and irrelevant to the bigger issues facing Americans in daily life, such as poverty, health care, education, and social justice. To act first and to state reality first, even in a tweet, is to create the new reality to which the public reacts, positively or negatively. Therefore the discourse obfuscates "real" reality and real issues. Overall, postmodern culture and postmodern media are not very good at ignoring the ridiculous in favor of the important. The first admittedly clever act of the Christian Right has been to take advantage of the postmodern climate of pluralism to create equivalency between the virtual and the real, the fake and the genuine, the extremely abstract and the most sincerely practical.

The second move of the Christian Right has been to use the climate of false equivalency that postmodernity tends to permit to repackage Christian faith and dogma as a set of facts worthy of the same authority granted to the discoveries of modern science. This is a deft and tricky, though I imagine unconscious, maneuver. It affirms both postmodernity and modernity simultaneously. This move uses postmodern pluralism to perform a bait and switch. The bait is pluralism and the argument that expressions of Christian faith are part of a balanced presentation of the facts; the switch comes when Christianity is understood in a modernist way as a factual description of reality. To present Christianity as a set of facts that competes with science is to ask a listener or reader to understand Christianity as a modern, objective, and authoritative epistemology. Postmodernity is the bait, and modern authoritative (though presumed) facts are the switch. Within this remarkable maneuver are misunderstandings of both postmodernity and modernity, but to know and identify these misunderstandings, one must have an education, and a decent public education is one thing the Christian Right has worked hard to undermine.[2]

Over against the Christian Right's perpetration of this abusive situation, mainline media and mainline scholarship in religion are only beginning to wake up. Some news agencies have raised problems with treating climate change and climate change denial as equivalent opinions. There is at least some indication that journalists need to think twice when interviewing political candidates who deny climate change.[3] Even the giant

2. The Christian Right uses the phrase "school choice" or "education choice" as a code word for privatizing education and undermining, perhaps even seeking to eliminate, the public-school system. According to the *Detroit Free Press* (Jennifer Dixon, June 22, 2014), with charter schools the Christian Right has succeeded only in providing poor education. Dixon reported that 38 percent of charter schools that received state academic ranking fell below the twenty-fifth percentile in rank. This contrasts with 23 percent of public schools. See Dixon, "Michigan Spends."

3. Hilzik, "How Should Journalists Treat Candidates Who Deny Climate Change?"

ExxonMobil Corporation, which had supported climate change denial, in 2008, chose to cut off funding to public policy groups that deny the over-whelming evidence of real science (remarkably this occurred when Rex Tillerson was chair and CEO of ExxonMobil).[4]

Postmodernity promised to liberate our culture from singular, authoritative, and isolated notions of the truth. It promised to, and has, opened and affirmed pluralism, and it upholds that the human interpreta-tion of reality is a dynamic, relational, constructive, and communal project. But postmodernity has also held a troubling side, which is noticeable in how the Christian Right has taken advantage. Postmodernity gives space in discourse to unfounded alternative views that, however misleading, require a fair hearing in the name of pluralism. Climate change denial is one such example. Unfortunately—as any modernist who still thinks there is something like truth might say—not all alternative views are equal in value. Some lack the modern requirement of evidence. Postmodernity is not against the modern requirement of evidence, but it has often over-looked this requirement in the name of personal experience. Sometimes this omission is appropriate, especially when "evidence" becomes some-thing privileged bodies hold and use to exploit those whom modernity has traditionally silenced or shunned; but other times this openness allows an opportunity to call real evidence fake and real science a hoax. This space of ambiguity that arose in the critique of modernity inadvertently gave the Christian Right opportunities to build its base on lost ideas of the modern past and on modernity's sense of ultimate truth.

The modern idea of truth assumed that objectivity or independent observation could raise to the surface deep elements of reality thought to be essential or universal. On the surface, for example, and at first glance, Christianity claims that the resurrection of the Christ promises a restored, final humanity. Modern theology attempted to understand this historically particular claim as a surface expression, bound in first-century cosmol-ogy, of a deeper truth. Modern theology, expressed in individuals like Re-inhold Niebuhr and Paul Tillich, could argue that human nature deludes itself through false desires of the ego (such as in consumerism), but we can find hints of the true self in deep spiritual mysteries encountered in the Christ. Paul Tillich expressed the ancient myth with profound modern sophistication when he defined the Christ event with the idea of existential

4. This information was reported in the *Guardian* (May 28, 2008). The *Guardian* in-dicated that much of the pressure to take this decision came from the Rockefeller family.

estrangement and New Being. Salvation is New Being. Tillich was radical and innovative, and pressed theology against philosophy and psychology, but he remained a "modern" figure because the emphasis with Tillich fell on an isolated and final truth that lay deeply hidden under the surfaces of Christian mythology and dogma. That sense of a final or ultimate reality gave to Tillich a sense of bedrock objectivity, which he could unearth from culturally relative and historic myths.

Postmodern theology feeds from Tillich but collapses his claims about ultimate reality. In postmodern thought, human nature is a construct, so claims that assume an essential quality to human nature are suspect. Human nature emerges from the social and political forces that open spaces of experience. Alternate spaces create alternate natures, but there is nothing sinister or deeply intentional about this. Human nature, in the postmodern sense, "happens"; it is happenstantial, as Don Cupitt might say.[5] As such, there is no ultimate realty or final essence to appeal to for existential resolution. Without an essence, a resolution is not needed. Without an essence, at the practical level, it is hard to argue that there are or should be fixed gender identities, fixed social roles for males and females, fixed economic systems, or fixed social values. Reality is fluid, and what "truth" might mean in one era or set of circumstances can differ vastly from what it may mean in another era or set of circumstances. The fear of the Christian Right is that such fluidity means that there is no objective truth, that all is permissible, and that no final authority is in charge. The appeal of Donald Trump to the Christian Right obviously has nothing to do with Trump's religious sentiments; it has a lot to do with his being male and his being (perceived as) the man in charge, the man who will set things right, the man who objectively names things as they are, and the man who will put the fake and fluid usurpers of "political correctness" back in their place. The Christian Right, though, is entirely wrong. Postmodernity is not the end of truth, the end of evidence, the end of reason, or the end of civilization. To be sure, postmodernity makes these modern principles more difficult to talk about and more suspect when employed authoritatively, but it does not signal the end of evidence-based reason holding more value to humanity than impression-based opinion.

Postmodernity exposed the myth of objectivity, both at the level of physics (starting with the Heisenberg principle) and in everyday human experience (with hermeneutical questions about place, power, and

5. Cupitt, *Emptiness and Brightness*.

subjectivity). Objectivity, which assumes isolated observation and nonparticipation, was succinctly rebuffed many years ago by Owen Barfield during the era of existentialism.[6] But as Barfield intuitively knew, objectivity still needs to be redeemed as something useful. To be sure, the myth of objectivity is a construct of social and linguistic dynamics that assume a technical worldview. Objectivity underestimates the complex and dynamically relative phenomena we call reality. Still, postmodern thought is communal and relational, which means that the integrity of reason, though open to critique and sometimes troubling, remains standing. Human beings communicate and construct their reality out of different cultures, languages, and experiences, but the postmodern affirmation of human construction involved in the real is not a denial of humanity itself or of the promise reason holds for cooperation at an international level. What is required is not a proclamation of ultimate truth but a willingness to embrace fluidity in debate and an effort to construct a just world.

Ironically, the Christian Right is more extreme in its "postmodernism" than those philosophers and theologians who gave birth to postmodern thought. The irony, though, is a troubled irony that must also be related to modernity and even to the Middle Ages. The Christian Right attempts to retrieve a stable and objective world and, for fear of fluidity and due to the natural assuaging power of stories from the past, to place that lost world in an objective position. Let us put this another way. Religion is about remembering forward. It is about telling heroic stories that lessen fear for the world and that motivate hearers to move forward into the adventure of life, confidently taking risks and seeking good practices. Religion, with its grand narratives and rituals of passage, attempts to tame the future whether by appeasing gods or reminding the agent of identity, heritage, and character. Religion is always moving forward; it is always the project of becoming human. But the religious Right aims religion backwards. The very fluidity that moves religion dynamically forward in ever new forms is turned around to focus all energy backward on a fictional past of stability. This focus on past times inevitably leads to a focus on the orders of past societies. The story no longer moves toward challenge, change, and new being; the story moves backward, to protect and justify past orders—whether an order is defined doctrinally (in religious laws and beliefs) or socially (as economic privileges and rank)—with authority supposed from either natural or eternal commandments.

6. Barfield, *Saving the Appearances*.

We can recall that the political term "Right" comes out of the composition of the Estates-General in France's old regime. On the left side of the president sat the representatives of the common people, and on the right sat the nobility. The noble class, with its high social status, large land holdings, and condescending sense of noblesse oblige, had little interest in or motivation to reform; the point of nobility is to keep things the same, the state of which is assumed to be the natural order, and to restrict the enhancement of society to the charity of its wealthy members. "Let them eat cake" is Marie Antoinette's often-misunderstood comment, but it is misunderstood because the hearers of that phrase were the common people who could only regard it as a flippant, callous comment that offered far less than what noblesse oblige requires.

We can see the mythic construct of noblesse oblige in action when viewing the Christian Right from a working-class perspective. The wealthy should be wealthy, according to the myth, for the benefit of the common good. Their hands should not be tied to money, since they have enough of it, but to unselfish social service and a vision for a better country; models of American noblesse oblige include Presidents Franklin Roosevelt and John F. Kennedy.[7] Both from wealthy backgrounds, they symbolized noblesse oblige in the traditional sense of serving one's country by answering the call of the common good. In the case of the Kennedy era, though, the rise of the middle class was coupled with the power of unions, higher taxation levels on wealth, and higher corporate tax rates. Taxes express the obligations of wealthier members of society to the common good. It is, after all, the common market that enables wealth. The Reagan administration took advantage of this historic sense of noblesse oblige to advance the idea that the wealthy need to be wealthier in order for the common good to be more common. It is both an odd idea and a weak argument. Practically, too, it does not work. When the rich get richer, there is less common money, which means that the poor can only get poorer.

The Donald Trump administration has advanced the Right with the assumption that what we need for the common good is more money concentrated in the hands of the wealthy to satisfy the requirements of noblesse oblige—though Trump does not use (and might be incapable of using) such

---

7. I had concluded some of these thoughts independently, and then found an excellent, popular article that reinforces some of these observations. See Mansur, "Donald Trump and *Noblesse Oblige* in Politics," *American Thinker* (July 28, 2016). Mansur wrote before the national election of 2016 but successfully predicted, in this article, the election of Donald Trump.

language. His platform addressed working-class America with the ringing cries of this myth. He would focus on and eliminate immigration policies that prevent honest Americans from getting jobs. He would restore the industrial complex so that American factories stayed in American and employed Americans. He would reopen the coal mines and restore labor in the oil and gas industry. He would make America great again. With such sloganism, and while appealing to the Right with nationalistic sentiments about persevering and respecting the sacredness of the (same old) social order, the Trump administration hoodwinked the masses (likely not deliberately because it has no such sophistication). What made America great in the past was labor unions that protected jobs, enhanced wages, ensured safety, and invested in families through education, health, and vacation benefits. The myth of past American greatness was certainly overstated, but that's politics. America was, though, arguably better in the sense that in the past it had fairer taxation and stronger unions. These two factors made it possible to have a growing middle class and to offer hope for advancement to those families who knew poverty. What is at stake in Trump's nationalism, and what rests on a hidden doctrine of noblesse oblige, is that this privileged doctrine, which seeks to dismantle the common good, appeals (or did appeal) surprisingly broadly to working-class America. The doctrine of wealth first and handouts later crushes national policies that serve the common good. Education becomes a limited commodity, and poverty expands its tragic presence among the masses. Somehow America, unlike its Western allies, seems incapable of addressing these fundamental and critical (indeed modern) issues. America seems willing to undermine itself with its own nationalism, which stymies self-criticism and casts a shadow of suspicion on genuine efforts to change.

Against a background of social and political stalemate, it is not immediately obvious how theology can make a difference. It might be the case that theology cannot—theology in the academic sense of a study of Christian history or doctrine or biblical texts. But theology is not limited to academic study. It also has a social dimension because it is also, beyond academics, a worldview. The Western world's "worldview" rests largely on Christian history and its secular dimensions. Christianity in its Western form, even in its most powerful expressions, has always left the sword (political power) in the hands of the state. The church has certainly been adept at blessing the sword, but it has rarely held it directly. Even on occasions when the church did hold the sword directly, in these instances the church was held in check by secular powers. What more directly concerns the church is the secular—that is, expressed Christian concern for the quality of life in the *saeculum,* or in our age. The gospel emphasis lies here with concern for the poor, the questioning of power, and the vision of a different social order. Jesus sayings related to these themes are found in practices such as open commensality[8] and in sayings that associate poverty with the empire of God.[9] It is, of course, anachronistic to associate social justice as we know it with the Jesus of history, but it is consistent to draw out from Christian history the gospel mission to the world expressed in compassion, equality, and liberation from poverty.[10]

These themes have always been present in Christian charity, especially in the establishment of hospitals and universities, and they emerged beyond mere charity in the acute and focused call for justice in the social gospel seeking "the kingdom of God on earth."[11] The point is that Christianity and its heritage of Jewish prophetic witness drive theology toward social ideals that resonate with the integrity of religion, and that can be realized in society now. What must change is the ideological center of the social understanding of religion, which is entirely possible. Christianity has an intimate history with health care and education; it is not unreasonable, and even more, it is appropriate, for "Christian" values to be defined by social medicine and free universities. Bernie Sanders, in his quest for the Democratic presidential nomination, made these two historic Christian and Jewish ideals his platform. They proved overwhelmingly popular with all but the Democratic Party establishment. The trick for Sanders, whether

8. Crossan, *Jesus,* 66ff.

9. "How happy are the poor" is a minor but consistent example of rising Christianity's memory that associated its birth with poverty and the empire of God.

10. These are present in well-known Christian phrases such as the Pauline "in Christ there is not male or female, slave or free," or the Lukan emphasis on proclaiming good news to the poor and release to the captives. The Jesus saying that congratulates the poor presumes an opportunity hidden to wealth, and the interesting teaching to "give to Caesar what Caesar deserves" raises an interesting question about what powerful figures like Caesar really deserve. The answer might be a revolution. My point here is that the aim of the Christian gospel, even while many insist its concern is heaven, has always and at the very least included the transformation of the earth.

11. This is perhaps as good a motto as can be found for the Social Gospel movement. The phrase was used by the "Brotherhood of the Kingdom" to which Walter Rauschenbusch belonged. Rauschenbusch made a good summary statement of his views on the aims of the gospel when he stated that "It is not a matter of getting individuals to heaven, but of transforming the life on earth into the harmony of heaven" (Rauschenbusch, *Christianity and the Social Crisis,* 65).

conscious or not, was to undermine the false notion that Christianity is about noblesse oblige and to reinstate Christianity's heart, which is justice.

Trumpian nationalism rests on the latent presence of noblesse oblige in the American psyche as a kind of relict of the French Revolution. It surfaces in the Christian Right with the basic idea that society is composed of individuals rather than communities, and that the solution to social ills is to buttress wealthy people and grow more poverty. It is, to be sure, a corrupted and lost understanding of noblesse oblige, but such is the legacy of that notion contorted by nationalism and politicized by fake Christians being born again in Trumpism. There are never perfect answers to problematic social questions. Reinhold Niebuhr wisely defined democracy as a proximate solution to insoluble problems.[12] There are, however, basic solutions to basic kinds of problems. Those solutions already exist and are already being demonstrated as constructive truths in health care policies, social welfare policies, education policies, and criminal justice policies enacted in other Western countries. In these other countries not far away, crime rates are lower, people live longer, education levels are higher, and a greater standard of living is enjoyed by a greater number of people. Nationalism combined with Christianity, cooked on the Right side and skewed with hidden values from past eras, serves a dish called Trumpism, in which all of the above is denied to the American people—but real Christianity and real Christians could, if the will is present, change the recipe.

12. Niebuhr, *Moral Man, Immoral Society.*

16

Eternal Scar of the Fictive Mind

Noëlle Vahanian

Let's say, with Plato, that all knowledge is recollection. How would this conception work for a radical materialism?

Then history would really be a work of fiction, for events defy the immutability of eternal being and, as new, events thus cannot be known or recalled.

I remember where I was the morning of 9/11, in my house apartment, Trinity Place, Syracuse, New York, glued to the television screen. But it was not written that this terrorist attack on U.S. soil should happen, albeit that such an idea to fly planes and to crash them into buildings had been imagined. One has only to look at child's play for that. I don't recall killing in my child's play, though as soon as I put this on paper, I do remember pretend-shooting my brother while playing gangsters and robbers. In what happened on 9/11, none of my recollecting is pure. I was not there, or in Manhattan. My view was from the camera lens, several of them. There was the newscaster, Ashley Banfield, with her thick rimmed glasses (did she have them yet, or did these come slightly later?). I was not a first responder; no one I knew died. But anyone who was there, close by, remembers that day in a way that would want to defy the notion that history is fiction. And what we mean by this is that those near remember this event in the flesh. Whether it be the smog or the smell or the sheer terror from the proximate horror; the seen, the felt, the experienced left an imprint, a traumatic scar.

That scar would be what of an event passes over into a realm of eternal objects to be recalled vividly or falsely, or even both.

So history is a work of fiction, but for the scars that it leaves in its making. They mark the passage of events in a quasi-indelible way. It is even possible one may genetically inherit trauma; that is, trauma is liable of being passed down, and this not merely through the scenario of the vicious circle, such as the one we might be aware of, which afflicts abusers and their victims, who, in turn, become abusers themselves. Quite possibly then, one's flesh has been so scarred—so traumatized—that one's genes hold markers that once passed down, when through various circumstances in the environment of the offspring, could be activated. The offspring, in turn, to appear to suffer from a traumatic experience, yet one which for the general population would not have been traumatic.

I went to the 9/11 Memorial & Museum. I saw what's left of the Twin Towers in the underground museum. A sense of the immense, awesome magnitude of the devastation is conveyed through the mere gigantism of the place, as if to say this is as devastating, as inconceivable, and as extraordinary as a holocaust—*this is a holocaust*. The main intent is to memorialize the victims whose lives ended in infernal agony. The museum, therefore, does not offer any substantive analysis of terrorism. It tells a story based on time lines. One can hear the last cell phone messages of victims to their loved ones; one can see footage of victims jumping from the burning towers. But of the attackers one learns little: that most were Saudis, that they were part of Osama bin Laden's extremist terrorist Al-Qaeda group, that the United States went into Afghanistan because the country was an Al-Qaeda terrorist haven. Through its silence or omission, the museum does not overtly correct the mistaken or misleading association of Iraq and the Saddam Hussein regime with 9/11 and Al-Qaeda. I may be wrong on that point. Though the clear impression left on the visitor is that the museum informs less on the nature of terrorism than it does on the experience of and response to the terror born of such an act of terrorism. And while we know that the nearly three thousand people who were killed in the coordinated attacks on that day came from ninety-three nations, we also come to understand how New Yorkers were immediate victims, while the World Trade Center and the Pentagon were symbolic targets standing for economic globalization and U.S. military power. One learns of the horrific ordeal people endured and of the heroism of first responders and ordinary people: volunteers, the New York Police Department, the Fire Department of the City of New York. The museum's architecture and multimedia presentations hallow ground zero, which becomes an underground virtual mausoleum to mark the notable absence of the gigantic towers from the cityscape. One leaves feeling somewhat abashed by the focus on the victims with whom one cannot help but identify or empathize—*our way of life was attacked*: what should this mean to the ordinary citizen?

Shop!

But the world over is reeling with victims. The Warsaw Rising Museum tells the story of the city's destruction during the Nazi German invasion of Poland—a city reduced to ashes. The museum memorializes the 1944 uprising, and it also recounts the difficult, oppressive years that followed under communist totalitarianism, until the city's rebirth with the fall of the Soviet bloc. Too often sidestepped in the pantheon of World War II's victims, Poles want the West to recognize their difficult plight, their double-victimization, and the museum identifies the resilience of those who held strong and resisted, over a fifty-year span, if all too often to their death, a human machinery of terror. Even the Washington DC Holocaust Memorial Museum, whose principal objective is to tell the story of the Holocaust from the end of the Weimar Republic to the Allied liberation—Nuremberg laws, Kristallnacht, ghettos, deportation to work camps, extermination camps—aims to prevent future genocides through education and awareness. Hiroshima's Memorial Museum aims for nuclear disarmament. The National Museum of the American Indian aims to demonstrate and celebrate "survivance"—even in the midst of the country's capital city, with a vegetable garden on the steps of the museum.

The 9/11 Memorial Museum aims to inform us about the state of terror on 9/11, and in this, it invites unity. But unity in what? As survivors? As fighters? As consumers? As patriots? I am not sure. The lesson is one of unity, no doubt—unity in the face of adversity. But unity in the middle of Manhattan means wearing commemorative, inspirational, and patriotic tees and caps, bracelets and pins, readily available through the museum's online gift shop. We're soon all wearing the lapel flag pin, a biopolitical corset to show that we are on the right side—ironically, the side of *freedom*. And in so doing, we conflate our humanism with an obscene nationalistic patriotism and its presumptuous exceptionalism: "if you don't think we are the best in the world, then you should leave." Even Obama wore the pin. Trump added the cap with the caption to tell all.

Thus it is that the 9/11 Memorial & Museum does nothing to prevent extremism, intolerance, or bigotry. But it does everything to rally up the troops under the flag. I am not impugning the museum though. I am pointing out in another way how when knowledge is recollection, history is fiction but for the scars. This is not just about remembrance; it is about the fiction that though 9/11 represents unthinkable evil, our resilience and spirit of unity is why nothing has really changed. Certainly everything has changed for those who lost loved ones. Certainly many still bear the wounds of trauma. Certainly that their life return to a semblance of normalcy was not a given. But really, for those who were not scarred, there was nothing to recollect but the *fiction*, the narrative we told ourselves to explain what happened.

There is a something indelible, and yet, it can be forgotten or silenced or denied or misrecognized. Wear a pin. Or a cap.

I am puzzled by how people can be so comfortable, so at ease in their tribalism. Their tunnel-vision is baffling. Their ignorance, their deafness to their own ignorance, their indifference to their ignorance, their certainty in it,—utterly discomfiting. "He says what everybody thinks: it IS a hell-hole country. We keep bailing them out, and look what they're doing with our help!" I cringe. What is there to say? "There are good people on both sides?!"

Yes, this is a good old adage. Even among our enemies there must be some good people. The white nationalist has his reasons for espousing his racist ideology and spewing hateful slogans. He's got a whole set of alternative facts to support his factless, made-up knowledge. So we're back to Galileo and the Church, bound for another revolution. Ticktock. The pendulum swings. The sun revolves around the earth, say the ones. The other way around, say the others. Could both be true? The question is cumbersome. Let's move on.

The morass of free speech without universals prevents easy vindication of either camp. Let me draw a parallel.

I know that the Armenian genocide happened. The Turkish nationalist does not—can't know by virtue of his identity, has to deny it or, simply, refuses to accept the "other" side's version. In his mind, the other side is spewing propaganda. It's a propaganda machine: a pro-Western, anti-Islam machine; it's more problematic because it's an Islamophobic machine trying to prevent Turkey from entering the European Union. Before that, it was a Soviet-backed machine. And before that, it was the British, imperialist-backed machine.

Well, in this world, it is difficult to detach reasons from geopolitical interests—from any interests, in general, as we know after reading Kant.

I know that systemic racism founds this nation, even in its adulation of its highest value—freedom. But the neighbor down the street has worked hard all his life. Where is his river of milk and honey? He thinks the inner city folk are up to no good and it's their own doing. He thinks the Mexicans are all here illegally taking his job. He thinks he's the victim. Give him a memorial! Now down south they want to take down confederate monuments. He finds this offensive. He is oblivious to the Lost Cause mythos to which many of these monuments owe their existence. If you try to explain it to him, he won't hear any of it. It's left-wing, liberal propaganda. He is infuriated by the NFL players' refusal to stand during the national anthem. If you explain to him that the protest aims to raise awareness about racial injustice and police brutality, he'll list the half a dozen cases of black on black crime or of loss of police life in the line of duty that he's heard of.

And you all wonder how Trump was elected? When history is fiction, that's how.

And if being is changing, then there is no knowing of it anyway, and its recollecting (recollecting of being) points to the limits of knowing oneself, one's history, one's culture.

Every seven years, my body is a new body, and yet it is aging all the same. I am born a blank slate, so much so that I don't even know that I am one who exists, and yet, my DNA is ancient.

And it is perhaps in this vein that the affirmation "I am a Christian" rings true—it aspires to the eternal.

Bibliography

Abu-Jamal, Mumia. *Writing on the Wall: Selected Prison Writings of Mumia Abu-Jamal.* Edited by Johanna Fernández. San Francisco: City Lights, 2015.
———. "Interview with the *Revolutionary Worker.*" December 1994. http://www.geocities.ws/liberonsmumia/interview.html.
Achen, Christopher H., and Larry M. Bartels. *Democracy for Realists: Why Elections Do Not Produce Responsive Government.* Princeton Studies in Political Behavior. Princeton: Princeton University Press, 2016.
Alberts, William. "American Churches: The 'Master Race' and 'American Exceptionalism.'" *Counterpunch*, February 22, 2016. http://www.counterpunch.org/2016/02/22/christian-churches-the-master-race-and-american-exceptionalism.
Albright, Madeleine. "My Undiplomatic Moment." *New York Times*, February 12, 2016. https://www.nytimes.com/2016/02/13/opinion/madeleine-albright-my-undiplomatic-moment.html.
Alexander, Joseph. *Christocracy: Christ's Kingdom Governance on Earth by True Followers.* Meadville PA: Christian Faith Publishing, 2018.
Alexander, Michelle. *The New Jim Crow: Mass Incarceration in the Age of Colorblindness.* New York: New Press, 2012.
Anti-Defamation League. "ADL Resource Identifies the Key Players of the Alt Right and Alt Lite." 2017. https://www.adl.org/news/press-releases/key-leaders-alt-right-vs-alt-lite.
"An Appeal for Theological Understanding: The Hartford Declaration." *Worldview* 18/4 (April 1, 1975). https://worldview.carnegiecouncil.org/archive/worldview/1975/04/2511.html.
Arendt, Hannah. *Essays in Understanding, 1930–1954: Formation, Exile, and Totalitarianism.* New York: Schocken, 1994.
Aslan, Reza. *Zealot: The Life and Times of Jesus of Nazareth.* New York: Random House, 2013.
Avalos, Hector. "The Ideology of the Society of Biblical Literature and the Demise of an Academic Profession." SBL Forum Archive. *Society of Biblical Literature.* April 14, 2006. http://sbl-site.org/Article.aspx?ArticleID=520.
Baker, Kelly J. *Gospel according to the Klan: The KKK's Appeal to Protestant America, 1915–1930.* Lawrence: University of Kansas Press, 2011.
Balmer, Randall. *Thy Kingdom Come: How the Religious Right Distorts Faith and Threatens America; An Evangelical's Lament.* New York: Basic Books, 2007. Kindle.

Balsiger, David W., dir. *George W. Bush: Faith in the White House.* Written by Sharon Dymmel and Joseph Miller. Produced by Grizzly Adams Productions Inc. DVD. New York: GoodTimes DVD, 2004.

Bardella, Kurt. "Say Goodbye to Your Republican Party." *CNN,* October 25, 2017. http://www.cnn.com/2017/10/24/opinions/goodbye-republican-party-opinion-bardella/index.html.

Barfield, Owen. *Saving the Appearances.* New York: Harcourt Brace Jovanovich, 1965.

Barghouti, Omar. *BDS: Boycott, Divestment, Sanctions; The Global Struggle for Palestinian Rights.* Chicago: Haymarket, 2011.

Barth, Karl. *The Epistle to the Romans.* Translated from the 6th ed. by Edwyn C. Hoskyns, bart., with a new preface by the author. 1933. London: Oxford University Press, 1968.

Bayat, Asef. *Life as Politics: How Ordinary People Change the Middle East.* 2nd ed. Stanford: Stanford University Press, 2013.

Berlant, Lauren. *Cruel Optimism.* Durham: Duke University Press, 2011.

Bessler, Joe. "In Trump the Republican Party Gets the Savior It Has Sought." *Nondoc,* December 28, 2015. https://nondoc.com/2015/12/28/in-trump-republican-party-gets-the-savior-it-has-sought.

Black, Amy E. "'Evangelicals, Politics, and Public Policy: Lessons from the Past, Prospects for the Future." In *The Future of Evangelicalism in America,* edited by Candy Gunther Brown and Mark Silk, 124–57. The Future of Religion in America. New York: Columbia University Press, 2016.

Bloch, Ernst. *The Principle of Hope.* Translated by Neville Plaice et al. 3 vols. Studies in Contemporary German Social Thought. 1st American ed. Cambridge: MIT Press, 1986.

Blum, Edward J. *Reforging the White Republic: Race, Religion, and American Nationalism, 1865–1898.* Conflicting Worlds. Baton Rouge: Louisiana State University Press, 2005.

———. *Reforging the White Republic: Race, Religion, and American Nationalism, 1865–1898.* Updated edition with a new foreword by John Stauffer. Louisiana paperback ed. Conflicting Worlds. Baton Rouge: Louisiana State University Press, 2015.

Boger, Julian. "'A Recipe for Scandal': Trump Conflicts of Interest Point to Constitutional Crisis." *Guardian,* November 27, 2016. https://www.theguardian.com/us-news/2016/nov/27/donald-trump-conflicts-interest-constitutional-crisis.

Bonhoeffer, Dietrich. *The Cost of Discipleship.* Rev. and unabridged [6th] ed. New York: Macmillan, 1963.

Bonilla-Silva, Eduardo. *Racism without Racists: Color-Blind Racism and the Persistence of Racial Inequality in America.* 5th ed. New York: Rowman & Littlefield, 2017.

Boym, Svetlana. "The Future of Nostalgia: From Cured Soldiers to Incurable Romantics." In *The Svetlana Boym Reader,* edited by Cristina Vatulescu et al., 217–76. London: Bloomsbury Academic, 2018. http://monumenttotransformation.org/atlas-of-transformation/html/n/nostalgia/nostalgia-svetlana-boym.html.

Brown, Candy Gunther, and Mark Silk, eds. *The Future of Evangelicalism in America.* The Future of Religion in America. New York: Columbia University Press, 2016.

Burke, Kenneth. *Language as Symbolic Action.* Berkeley: University of California Press, 1966.

Butler, Judith. "Judith Butler's Remarks to Brooklyn College on BDS." *Nation,* February 7, 2013. https://www.thenation.com/article/judith-butlers-remarks-to-brooklyn-college-bds.

BIBLIOGRAPHY

Caputo, John D. *What Would Jesus Deconstruct? The Good News of Postmodernity for the Church.* The Church and Postmodern Culture. Grand Rapids: Baker Academic, 2007.

Castells, Manuel. *The Rise of the Network Society.* 2nd ed., with a new preface. The Information Age: Economy, Society, and Culture 1. Malden, MA: Wiley-Blackwell, 2010.

CBN News. World. "'We Want God': President Trump Defends Faith, Family, Freedom in Poland Speech." July 6, 2017. *CBN News* (website). http://www1.cbn.com/cbnnews/world/2017/july/we-want-god-president-trump-defends-faith-family-freedom-in-poland-speech.

Chidester, David. *Empire of Religion: Imperialism and Comparative Religion.* Chicago: University of Chicago Press, 2014.

Cillizza, Chris. "The 12 Most Damning Bob Corker Quotes about Donald Trump." CNN Politics. The Point with Chris Cillizza. *CNN*, October 9, 2017. https://www.cnn.com/2017/10/09/politics/trump-corker-quotes/index.html.

Cohen, Zachary, and Richard Roth. "UN Passes Fresh Sanctions on North Korea." CNN Politics. *CNN*, September 12, 2017. http://www.cnn.com/2017/09/11/politics/north-korea-un-security-council-vote/index.html.

Collins, Kaitlin. "Trump Repeats Equivocal Charlottesville Rhetoric after Meeting with Black Senator." Politics. *CNN*, Sept. 14, 2017. http://www.cnn.com/2017/09/14/politics/trump-antifa-charlottesville-tim-scott/index.html.

Cone, James H. *The Cross and the Lynching Tree.* Maryknoll, NY: Orbis, 2011.

Connolly, William E. *Aspirational Fascism: The Struggle for Multifaceted Democracy under Trump.* Forerunners: Ideas First from the University of Minnesota Press. Minneapolis: University of Minnesota Press, 2017.

———. *Capitalism and Christianity, American Style.* Durham: Duke University Press, 2008.

———. *The Fragility of Things: Self-Organizing Processes, Neoliberal Fantasies, and Democratic Activism.* Durham: Duke University Press, 2013.

———. *Why I Am Not a Secularist.* Minneapolis: University of Minnesota Press, 1999.

Cook, John Granger. *Crucifixion in the Mediterranean World.* Wissenschaftliche Untersuchungen zum Neuen Testament 327. Tübingen: Mohr/Siebeck, 2014.

Coulthard, Glen Sean. *Red Skin, White Masks: Rejecting the Colonial Politics of Recognition.* Indigenous Americas. Minneapolis: University of Minnesota Press, 2014.

Cox, Daniel, and Robert P. Jones. "America's Changing Religious Identity." *Public Religion Research Institute*, Sept. 6, 2017. https://www.prri.org/research/american-religious-landscape-christian-religiously-unaffiliated.

Crenshaw, Kimberlé Williams. "Kimberlé Crenshaw on Intersectionality: 'I wanted to come up with an everyday metaphor that anyone could use.'" *New Statesman America* (April 2, 2014): https://www.newstatesman.com/lifestyle/2014/04/kimberl-crenshaw-intersectionality-i-wanted-come-everyday-metaphor-anyone-could.

———. *On Intersectionality: Essential Writings.* New York: New Press, forthcoming.

Criss, Doug. "5 Things for September 15: London Train Blast, North Korea, Trump, Irma, Immigration." 5 Things. *CNN*, September 15, 2017. http://www.cnn.com/2017/09/15/us/five-things-september-15-trnd/index.html.

Crockett, Clayton. *Radical Political Theology: Religion and Politics after Liberalism.* Insurrections: Critical Studies in Religion, Politics, and Culture. New York: Columbia University Press, 2011.

Crossan, John Dominic. *Jesus: A Revolutionary Biography*. New York: HarperSanFrancisco, 1994.

Cupitt, Don. *Emptiness and Brightness*. Santa Rosa, CA: Polebridge, 2001.

Davis, Angela Y. "Police, Prisons and the Neoliberal State." People's Assembly 3. Temple University, Philadelphia PA. January 9, 2016. https://www.youtube.com/watch?v=T6B6BFyGUIQ.

Deloria, Vine, Jr. *God Is Red: A Native View of Religion*. 3rd ed. Golden, CO: Fulcrum, 2003.

DeMar, Gary. "The Old and New Jerry Falwell." On *American Vision* (blog). May 21, 2007. https://americanvision.org/1288/old-jerry-falwell.

DeVega, Chauncey. "Can We Finally Kill off the Zombie Lie? Trump's Voters Mostly Weren't the 'White Working Class.'" *Salon*, June 6, 2017. https://www.salon.com/2017/06/07/can-we-finally-kill-off-the-zombie-lie-trumps-voters-mostly-werent-the-white-working-class.

———. "Donald Trump Has Dropped the GOP's Mask: Conservatism and Racism Officially the Same Thing." *Salon*, March 1, 2016. https://www.salon.com/2016/03/01/donald_trump_has_dropped_the_gops_mask_conservatism_and_racism_now_officially_the_same_thing.

———. "It Was the Racism, Stupid: Explaining Trump's Win Using White Working-Class 'Economic Anxiety' Is Just Wrong." *Alternet*, January 5, 2017. https://www.alternet.org/election-2016/white-working-class-lie.

Dijck, José van. *The Culture of Connectivity: A Critical History of Social Media*. Oxford: Oxford University Press, 2013.

Dixon, Jennifer. "Michigan Spends $1B on Charter Schools but Fails to Hold Them Accountable." *Detroit Free Press*, June 22, 2014. Updated January 16, 2017. https://www.freep.com/story/news/local/michigan/2014/06/22/michigan-spends-1b-on-charter-schools-but-fails-to-hold/77155074.

Djupe, Paul A., et al. "How Fights over Trump Have Led Evangelicals to Leave Their Churches." Monkey Cage. *Washington Post*, April 11, 2017. https://www.washingtonpost.com/news/monkey-cage/wp/2017/04/11/yes-many-voters-left-their-congregations-over-trump-so-what-else-is-new/?utm_term=.07ed918954b1.

Dorrien, Gary. *Social Ethics in the Making: Interpreting an American Tradition*. Oxford: Wiley-Blackwell, 2010.

Douglas, Kelly Brown. *Stand Your Ground: Black Bodies and the Justice of God*. Maryknoll, NY: Orbis, 2015.

Drury, Shadia B. *Leo Strauss and the American Right*. New York: St. Martin's, 1997.

Du Bois, W. E. B. *The Souls of Black Folk*. Edited with an introduction and notes by Brent Hayes Edwards. Oxford World's Classics. Oxford: Oxford University Press, 2007.

Dunbar-Ortiz, Roxanne. *An Indigenous Peoples' History of the United States*. ReVisioning American History. Boston: Beacon, 2014.

Durgin, Celina. "The Definitive Roundup of Trump's Scandals and Business Failures." *National Review*, March 16, 2016. http://www.nationalreview.com/article/432826/donald-trumps-scandals-and-business-failures-roundup.

Dussel, Enrique. *Ethics of Liberation in the Age of Globalization and Exclusion*. Translation edited by Alejandro A. Vallega. Translated by Eduardo Mendieta et al. Latin America Otherwise: Languages, Nations, Empires. Durham: Duke University Press, 2013.

Electronic Intifada. "Anti-BDS Laws." Webpage. January 22, 2018. https://electronicintifada.net/tags/anti-bds-laws.

Ellacuría, Ignacio. "The Crucified People: An Essay in Historical Soteriology." In *Ignacio Ellacuría: Essays on History, Liberation, and Salvation*, 195–225. Edited with an Introduction by Michael E. Lee. Commentary by Kevin F. Burke SJ. Maryknoll, NY: Orbis, 2013.

Evans, Rachel Held. *Searching for Sunday: Loving, Leaving, and Finding the Church*. Nashville: Nelson, 2015.

Farzan, Antonia Noori. "Motel 6 Locations in Phoenix Share Guest Lists with ICE Agents." Interview by Ari Shapiro. *All Things Considered*, NPR. September 15, 2017. http://www.npr.org/2017/09/15/551339907/motel-6-locations-in-phoenix-share-guest-lists-with-ice-agents.

Farzan, Antonia Noori, and Joseph Flaherty. "Attorneys Suspect Motel 6 Calling ICE on Undocumented Guests." *PheonixNewTimes.com*, September 13, 2017. http://www.phoenixnewtimes.com/news/motel-6-calling-ice-undocumented-guests-phoenix-immigration-lawyers-9683244.

Fifield, James. "Development of the Local Church." *Record of Christian Work* 11 (1900) 817–18.

Findlay, James F. *Dwight L. Moody: American Evangelist, 1837–1899*. 1969. Reprint, Eugene, OR: Wipf & Stock, 2007.

Finkelstein, Norman G. "Is the Occupation Legal?" In *Gaza: An Inquest into Its Martyrdom*, 367–408. Oakland: University of California Press, 2018.

Fisher, Mark. "Exiting the Vampire Castle." November 22, 2013. http://www.thenorthstar.info/?p=11299.

FitzGerald, Frances. *The Evangelicals: The Struggle to Shape America*. New York: Simon & Schuster, 2017.

Flake, Jeff. "My Party Is in Denial about Donald Trump." *Politico*, July 31, 2017. https://www.politico.com/magazine/story/2017/07/31/my-party-is-in-denial-about-donald-trump-215442.

Frank, Thomas. *What's the Matter with Kansas? How Conservatives Won the Heart of America*. 1st Owl Books ed. New York: Holt, 2005.

Friedman, Uri. "What Is a Populist? And Is Donald Trump One?" *The Atlantic* February 27, 2017. https://www.theatlantic.com/international/archive/2017/02/what-is-populist-trump/516525.

Funk, Robert, et al. *The Five Gospels: The Search for the Authentic Words of Jesus*. San Francisco: HarperSanFrancisco, 1993.

Gay, Roxanne. "No One Is Coming to Save Us from Trump's Racism." *New York Times*, January 12, 2018. https://www.nytimes.com/2018/01/12/opinion/trump-shithole-countries-haiti-el-salvador-african-countries-immigration-racism.html?_r=0.

George, Carol V. R. *God's Salesman: Norman Vincent Peale & the Power of Positive Thinking*. Religion in America Series. New York: Oxford University Press, 1993.

Gerson, Michael. "Conservative Mind Has Become Diseased." Opinions. *Washington Post*, May 25, 2017. https://www.washingtonpost.com/opinions/the-conservative-mind-has-become-diseased/2017/05/25/523f0964-4159-11e7-9869-bac8b446820a_story.html?utm_term=.a09c1c92bc6e.

Gloedge, Timothy E. W. *Guaranteed Pure: The Moody Bible Institute, Business, and the Making of Modern Evangelicalism*. Chapel Hill: University of North Carolina Press, 2015.

Gold, Hadas. "Megyn Kelly: Jesus and Santa Were White." *Politico*, December 12, 2013. https://www.politico.com/blogs/media/2013/12/megyn-kelly-jesus-and-santa-were-white-179491.

Goodman, Amy. "Joshua Green on the Devil's Bargain." Interview with Joshua Green. *Democracy Now!* July 26, 2017. https://www.democracynow.org/2017/7/26/joshua_green_on_the_devils_bargain.

Gordon, Avery F. *Ghostly Matters: Haunting and the Sociological Imagination*. New University of Minnesota Press ed. Minneapolis: University of Minnesota Press, 2008

———. *The Hawthorn Archive: Letters for the Utopian Margins*. New York: Fordham University Press, 2018.

Green, Emma. "It Was Cultural Anxiety That Drove White, Working-Class Voters to Trump." Politics. *The Atlantic*, May 9, 2017. https://www.theatlantic.com/politics/archive/2017/05/white-working-class-trump-cultural-anxiety/525771.

Green, James. *Death in the Haymarket: A Story of Chicago, the First Labor Movement, and the Bombing that Divided Gilded Age America*. New York: Anchor, 2007.

Gushee, David P. *Still Christian: Following Jesus out of American Evangelicalism*. Louisville: Westminster John Knox, 2017.

Hafner, Josh. "Is 'Pocahontas' a Racial Slur? Eric Trump Defends His Dad, but Native Americans Say Otherwise." *USA Today*, November 28, 2017. https://www.usatoday.com/story/news/nation-now/2017/11/28/pocahontas-racist-eric-trump-defends-his-dad-but-native-americans-say-otherwise/902837001.

Haidt, Jonathan. *The Righteous Mind: Why Good People Are Divided by Politics and Religion*. New York: Vintage, 2013.

Harney, Stefano, and Fred Moten. *The Undercommons: Fugitive Planning & Black Study*. Wivenhoe, NY: Minor Compositions, 2013.

Hartman, Saidiya V. *Lose Your Mother: A Journey along the Atlantic Slave Route*. New York: Farrar, Straus & Giroux, 2008.

Haselby, Sam. *The Origins of American Religious Nationalism*. Religion in America Series. New York: Oxford University Press, 2015.

Haymes, Stephen Nathan et al., eds. *The Routledge Handbook of Poverty in the United States*. Routledge Handbooks. New York: Routledge, 2017.

The Hill. "Transcript: Flake Announces Retirement from Senate Floor." October 24, 2017. http://thehill.com/homenews/senate/356932-transcript-flake-announces-retirement-from-senate-floor.

Hilzik, Michael. "How Should Journalists Treat Candidates Who Deny Climate Change?" *Los Angeles Times*, March 24, 2015. http://www.latimes.com/business/hiltzik/la-fi-mh-how-should-reporters-treat-candidates-who-deny-climate-change-20150324-column.html.

Hogue, Michael S. *American Immanence: Democracy for an Uncertain World*. Insurrections: Critical Studies in Religion, Politics, and Culture. New York: Columbia University Press, 2018.

Holmes, Jonathan. "The Legacy of Fallujah." *Guardian*, April 4, 2007. *Global Policy Forum*. https://www.globalpolicy.org/component/content/article/168/36353.html.

Horsley, Richard A. *Jesus and Empire: The Kingdom of God and the New World Disorder*. Minneapolis: Fortress, 2005.

Hout, Michael, and Claude S. Fischer. "Why More Americans Have No Religious Preference: Politics and Generations." *American Sociological Review* 2 (2002) 165–91.

Indivisible. "Introduction to the Guide." *Indivisible.com*, https://www.indivisible.org/guide.

James, William. "The Philippine Question." Proceedings of the Fifth Annual Meeting of the New England Anti-Imperialist League. December 1903. In *William James: Writings 1902–1910*, edited by Bruce Kucklick, 1130–35. New York: Literary Classics of the United States, 1987.

Johnson, Chalmers A. *Blowback: The Costs and Consequences of American Empire*. The American Empire Project. New York: Holt, 2004.

———. *Nemesis: The Last Days of the American Republic*. A Holt Paperback. The American Empire Project. New York: Metropolitan, 2006.

———. *The Sorrows of Empire: Militarism, Secrecy, and the End of the Republic*. The American Empire Project. New York: Holt, 2005.

Jones, Robert P. "Donald Trump and the Transformation of White Evangelicals." *Time*, November 19, 2016. http://time.com/4577752/donald-trump-transformation-white-evangelicals.

———. "How 'Values Voters' Became 'Nostalgia' Voters." *The Atlantic*, February 23, 2016. https://www.theatlantic.com/politics/archive/2016/02/the-trump-revelation/470559.

Kahl, Brigitte. *Galatians Re-Imagined: Reading with the Eyes of the Vanquished*. Paul in Critical Contexts. Minneapolis: Fortress, 2010.

Kammen, Michael G. *Mystic Chords of Memory: The Transformation of Tradition in American Culture*. New York: Vintage, 1991. Kindle.

Keller, Catherine. *Apocalypse Now and Then: A Feminist Guide to the End of the World*. 1996. Reprint, Minneapolis: Fortress, 2004.

———. *Cloud of the Impossible: Negative Theology and Planetary Entanglement*. Insurrections: Critical Studies in Religion, Politics, and Culture. New York: Columbia University Press, 2014.

———. *Face of the Deep: A Theology of Becoming*. London: Routledge, 2003.

———. *On the Mystery: Discerning Divinity in Process*. Minneapolis: Fortress, 2008.

———. *Political Theology of the Earth: Our Plantary Emergency and the Struggle for a New Public*. Insurrections: Critical Studies in Religion, Politics, and Culture. New York: Columbia University Press, 2018.

Kendi, Ibram X. *Stamped from the Beginning: The Definitive History of Racist Ideas in America*. New York: Nation, 2016.

King, Martin Luther, Jr. *The Papers of Martin Luther King, Jr.* Vol. 6, *Advocate of the Social Gospel: September 1948—March 1963*. Edited by Clayborne Carson. 7 vols. Berkeley: University of California Press, 2007.

———. "A Time to Break the Silence." In *A Testament of Hope: The Essential Writings and Speeches of Martin Luther King Jr.*, edited by James M. Washington, 231–44. New York: HarperCollins, 1991.

Klein, Naomi. *No Is Not Enough: Resisting Trump's Shock Politics and Winning the World We Need*. Chicago: Haymarket, 2017.

———. *The Shock Doctrine: The Rise of Disaster Capitalism*. New York: Picador, 2008.

Kristeva, Julia. *Revolution in Poetic Language*. Translated by Margaret Waller. With an introduction by Leon S. Roudiez. New York: Columbia University Press, 1984.

Kruse, Kevin M. *One Nation under God: How Corporate America Invented Christian America*. New York: Basic Books, 2015.

Lambert, Frank. *Religion in American Politics: A Short History*. Princeton: Princeton University Press, 2008.

La Monica, Paul R. "No Worries on Wall Street. Dow Hits New High," Money. *CNN*, September 15, 2017. http://money.cnn.com/2017/09/15/investing/stocks-market-dow-record-high/index.html.

Landers, Elizabeth, and James Masters. "Trump Retweets Anti-Muslim Videos." CNN Politics. *CNN*, November 30, 2017. https://www.cnn.com/2017/11/29/politics/donald-trump-retweet-jayda-fransen/index.html.

Lee, Deborah Jian. *Rescuing Jesus: How People of Color, Women & Queer Christians Are Reclaiming Evangelicalism*. Boston: Beacon, 2015.

————. "Why the Young Religious Right Is Leaning Left." *Time*, October 20, 2015. http://time.com/4078909/evangelical-millennials.

Lieven, Anatol. *America Right or Wrong: An Anatomy of American Nationalism*. Oxford: Oxford University Press, 2007.

Lincoln, Bruce. *Religion, Empire, and Torture: The Case of Achaemenian Persia, with a Postscript on Abu-Ghraib*. Chicago: University of Chicago Press, 2007.

Lipka, Michael. "Millennials Increasingly Are Driving Growth of 'Nones.'" FactTank: News in the Numbers. *Pew Research Center*, May 12, 2015. http://www.pewresearch.org/fact-tank/2015/05/12/millennials-increasingly-are-driving-growth-of-nones.

Lofton, Kathryn. "Understanding Is Dangerous." Politics. *The Point*. November 4, 2016. https://thepointmag.com/2016/politics/understanding-is-dangerous.

Lopez, Davina C. *Apostle to the Conquered: Reimagining Paul's Mission*. Paul in Critical Contexts. Minneapolis: Fortress, 2010.

Lucas, James A. "U.S. Has Killed More than 20 Million People in 37 'Victim Nations' since World War II." *Global Research: Centre for Research on Globalization*. January 7, 2018. https://www.globalresearch.ca/us-has-killed-more-than-20-million-people-in-37-victim-nations-since-world-war-ii/5492051.

Mangum, R. Todd, and Mark S. Sweetnam. *The Scofield Bible: Its History and Impact on the Evangelical Church*. Colorado Springs: Paternoster, 2009.

Mansur, Salim. "Donald Trump and *Noblesse Oblige* in Politics." *American Thinker*, July 28, 2016. https://www.americanthinker.com/articles/2016/07/donald_trump_and_emnoblesse_obligeem_in_politics.html.

Marazzi, Christian. *The Violence of Financial Capitalism*. Translated by Kristina Lebedeva and Jason Francis McGimsey. New ed. Semiotext(e) Intervention Series 2. Los Angeles: Semiotext(e), 2011.

Marty, Martin E. *Righteous Empire: The Protestant Experience in America*. Two Centuries of American Life: A Bicentennial Series. New York: Dial, 1970.

Mathewes, Charles. "White Christianity Is in Big Trouble. And It's Its Own Biggest Threat." *Washington Post*, December 19, 2017. https://www.washingtonpost.com/news/posteverything/wp/2017/12/19/white-christianity-is-in-big-trouble-and-its-its-own-biggest-threat/?utm_term=.8eda53b40ca3&wpisrc=nl_most&wpmm=1.

May, Charlie. "Liberals Were Right: Racism Played a Larger Role in Trump's Win Than Income and Authoritarianism." *Salon*, April 17, 2017. https://www.salon.com/2017/04/17/liberals-were-right-racism-played-a-larger-role-in-trumps-victory-than-income-inequality-and-authoritarianism.

Mbembe, Achlle. "Necropolitics." Translated by Libby Meintjes. *Public Culture* 15 (2003) 11–40.

McElwee, Sean, and Jason McDaniel. "Economic Anxiety Didn't Make People Vote for Trump, Racism Did." *Nation,* May 8, 2017. https://www.thenation.com/article/economic-anxiety-didnt-make-people-vote-trump-racism-did.

Meixler, Eli. "'It's Time to Wake Up.' Read John McCain's Speech to Naval Academy Graduates." *Time*, October 31, 2017. http://time.com/5003525/john-mccain-naval-academy-speech.

Memmi, Albert. *The Colonizer and the Colonized.* New York: Orion, 1965.

Mercadante, Linda A. *Belief without Borders: Inside the Minds of the Spiritual but Not Religious.* Oxford: Oxford University Press, 2014.

Merritt, Jonathan. "Trump Reveals the End of the Religious Right's Preeminence." *The Atlantic,* February 27, 2016. https://www.theatlantic.com/politics/archive/2016/02/the-demise-of-conservative-christian-political-prominence/471093.

Mignolo, Walter D. *Local Histories/Global Designs: Coloniality, Subaltern Knowledges, and Border Thinking.* Princeton Studies in Culture/Power/History. Princeton: Princeton University Press, 2000.

Miller, Daniel D. "The Mystery of Evangelical Trump Support?" *Constellations: An International Journal of Critical and Democratic Theory,* March 24, 2018. DOI: https://doi.org/10.1111/1467-8675.12351.

———. *The Myth of Normative Secularism: Religion and Politics in the Democratic Homeworld.* Pittsburgh: Duquesne University Press, 2016.

Moody, Dwight L. "Dynamite or Gospel." *Record of Christian Work*, October 1885, 1–2.

———. *Secret Power: The Secret of Success in Christian Life and Christian Work.* Chicago: Revel, 1881.

Moreno, Carolina. "9 Outrageous Things Donald Trump Has Said about Latinos." Latino Voices. *Huffington Post.* August 31, 2015. http://www.huffingtonpost.com/entry/9-outrageous-things-donald-trump-has-said-about-latinos_us_55e483a1e4b0c818f618904b.

Morrison, Toni. *Beloved.* New York: Plume, 1988.

———. "Mourning for Whiteness." In *Aftermath: Sixteen Writers on Trump's America. The New Yorker,* November 21, 2016. https://www.newyorker.com/magazine/2016/11/21/aftermath-sixteen-writers-on-trumps-america.

Mouffe, Chantal. *The Return of the Political.* London: Verso, 2005.

Mouw, Rachel J. "Hartford: A Reminiscence." *First Things*, April 28, 2015. https://www.firstthings.com/web-exclusives/2015/04/hartford-a-reminiscence.

Moyers, Bill. Interview with James Cone. *Bill Moyers: The Journal.* November 23, 2007. http://billmoyers.com/content/james-cone-on-the-cross-and-the-lynching-tree.

MSNBC. "Defense Secretary Mattis Visits South Korea Transcript 10/26/17." *Hardball with Chris Matthews.* http://www.msnbc.com/transcripts/hardball/2017-10-26.

Mudde, Cas, and Cristobal Rovira Kaltwasser. *Populism: A Very Short Introduction.* Very Short Introductions. New York: Oxford University Press, 2017.

Nagle, Angela. *Kill All Normies: Online Culture Wars from 4Chan and Tumblr to Trump and the Alt-Right.* Alresford, UK: Zero, 2017.

Nelson, Sophia. "What's Trump's Problem with Black Women?" *NBC News,* October 26, 2017. https://www.nbcnews.com/news/us-news/ag-sessions-says-trump-administration-pull-back-police-department-civil-n726826.

Neshoba Democrat. Transcript of Ronald Reagan's 1980 Neshoba County Fair Speech. *Neshoba Democrat*, November 15, 2007. http://neshobademocrat.com/Content/

NEWS/News/Article/Transcript-of-Ronald-Reagan-s-1980-Neshoba-County-Fair-speech/2/297/15599.

Newman, Saul. *Political Theology: A Critical Introduction.* Cambridge: Polity, 2018.

Nicolaou, Corinna. *A None's Story: Searching for Meaning inside Christianity, Judaism, Buddhism & Islam.* New York: Columbia University Press, 2016.

Niebuhr, Reinhold. *Moral Man and Immoral Society: A Study in Ethics and Politics.* New York: Scribner, 1932. Reprint, 1946.

Noll, Mark A. *The Civil War as a Theological Crisis.* The Steven and Janice Brose Lectures in the Civil War Era. Chapel Hill: University of North Carolina Press, 2006.

Office of Governor Andrew Cuomo. "Governor Cuomo Deploys National Guard and State Police to the U.S. Virgin Islands after Touring Hurricane Irma Damage." *Governor. NY.gov,* September 15, 2017, https://www.governor.ny.gov/news/governor-cuomo-deploys-national-guard-and-state-police-us-virgin-islands-after-touring.

Orwell, George. "Notes on Nationalism" (1945). http://orwell.ru/library/essays/nationalism/english/e_nat.

Pally, Marcia. *The New Evangelicals: Expanding the Vision of the Common Good.* Grand Rapids: Eerdmans, 2011.

Pappé, Ilan. *The Ethnic Cleansing of Palestine.* Oxford: Oneworld, 2006.

Park, Andrew Sung. *The Wounded Heart of God: The Asian Concept of Han and the Christian Doctrine of Sin.* Nashville: Abingdon, 1993.

Pew Research Center. Polling and Analysis. "Faith in Flux: Changes in Religious Affiliation in the U.S." April 27, 2007, revised February 2011. http://www.pewforum.org/2009/04/27/faith-in-flux.

———. *Religious Landscape Study 2015.* "Evangelical Protestants." http://www.pewforum.org/religious-landscape-study/religious-tradition/evangelical-protestant.

———. *Religious Landscape Study 2015.* "Generational Cohort." http://www.pewforum.org/religious-landscape-study/generational-cohort.

Phillips, Kevin. *American Theocracy: The Peril and Politics of Radical Religion, Oil, and Borrowed Money in the 21st Century.* New York: Viking, 2006.

———. *The Emerging Republican Majority.* With a new preface by the author. The James Madison Library in American Politics. Princeton: Princeton University Press, 2015.

Pierce, Charles S. "Roy Moore Is Exactly What the Republican Party Is All About." *Esquire,* November 10, 2017. http://www.esquire.com/news-politics/politics/a13518962/roy-moore-is-who-republicans-are.

Pietsch, B. M. *Dispensational Modernism.* Oxford: Oxford University Press, 2015.

Piketty, Thomas. *Capital in the Twenty-First Century.* Translated by Arthur Goldhammer. Cambridge: Belknap, 2014.

Politico. "Full Text: Donald Trump 2016 RNC Draft Speech Transcript." July 21, 2016. https://www.politico.com/story/2016/07/full-transcript-donald-trump-nomination-acceptance-speech-at-rnc-225974.

Posner, Sarah. "With God on His Side." *American Prospect,* October 23, 2005. http://prospect.org/article/god-his-side.

———. "Why Donald Trump's Glitzy Style Is Attracting Evangelical Voters." Acts of Faith. *Washington Post,* February 22, 2017. https://www.washingtonpost.com/news/acts-of-faith/wp/2016/02/22/why-donald-trumps-glitzy-style-is-attracting-evangelical-voters/?utm_term=.21f055f8bffb.

Prashad, Vijay. *Arab Spring, Libyan Winter.* Oakland, CA: AK Press, 2012.

Prothero, Stephen. "The Huge Cultural Shift That's Helping Trump Win Evangelicals." *Politico Magazine,* March 13, 2016. http://www.politico.com/magazine/story/2016/03/the-huge-cultural-shift-thats-helping-trump-win-evangelicals-213729.

Putnam, Robert D., and David E. Campbell. *American Grace: How Religion Divides and Unites Us.* New York: Simon & Schuster, 2010.

Rah, Soong-Chan. *The Next Evangelicalism: Releasing the Church from Western Cultural Captivity.* Downers Grove, IL: InterVarsity, 2009.

Rauschenbusch, Walter. *Christianity and the Social Crisis.* 1907. Reprint, Eugene, OR: Wipf & Stock, 2003.

Religion News Service. "Religious Groups Issue Statements on War with Iraq." March 19, 2003. http://www.pewforum.org/2003/03/19/publicationpage-aspxid616.

Reynolds, Simon, and Joy Press. *The Sex Revolts: Gender, Rebellion, and Rock 'n' Roll.* Cambridge: Harvard University Press, 1996.

Rivera Pagán, Luis N. *A Violent Evangelism: The Religious and Political Conquest of the Americas.* Westminster John Knox, 1992.

Robbins, Jeffrey W. *Radical Democracy and Political Theology.* Insurrections: Critical Studies in Religion, Politics, and Culture. New York: Columbia University Press, 2011.

Rosenwaltd, Brian. "After Charlottesville Republicans Must Grapple with Their History on Race." *Washington Post,* August 14, 2017. https://www.washingtonpost.com/news/made-by-history/wp/2017/08/14/after-charlottesville-republicans-must-grapple-with-their-history-on-race/?utm_term=.6a3d42fd9828.

Rubin, Jennifer. "Younger Evangelicals Give Us Reason for Hope." Opinons. Right Turn. *Washington Post* August 8, 2017. https://www.washingtonpost.com/blogs/right-turn/wp/2017/08/08/younger-evangelicals-give-us-reason-for-hope/?utm_term=.7306226ocb40.

Said, Edward. *Covering Islam: How the Media and the Experts Determine How We See the Rest of the World.* Rev. ed. Updated and with a new introduction by the author. New York: Vintage, 1997.

Schmitt, Carl. *The Concept of the Political.* Translated by George Schwab. Expanded ed. Chicago: University of Chicago Press, 2007.

———. *Political Theology: Four Chapters on the Concept of Sovereignty.* Chicago: University of Chicago Press, 2005.

Schrade, Brad. "Ga. College Linked to Klan Rituals Apologizes for 'Pain' of Its History." *Atlanta Journal-Constitution,* June 22, 2017. http://www.ajc.com/news/breaking-news/college-linked-klan-rituals-apologizes-for-pain-its-history/nYbpXM8wKncDM6AMv9VkKK.

———. "Macon's Women's College Seeks to Atone for Ku Klux Klan's Legacy." *Atlanta Journal-Constitution,* June 22, 2017. http://www.myajc.com/news/state--regional/macon-women-college-seeks-atone-for-klux-klan-legacy/.g7C2fxlEtmmV7ge4f7znCK.

Scofield, C. I. *Addresses on Prophecy.* Chicago: Bible Truth Depot, 1914.

Sharpe, Christina Elizabeth. *In the Wake: On Blackness and Being.* Durham: Duke University Press 2016.

Shepard, Steven. "Study: Views on Immigration, Muslims, Drove White Voters to Trump." *Politico,* June 13, 2017. https://www.politico.com/story/2017/06/13/trump-white-voters-immigration-muslims-239446.

Sloboda, John. "100 Names of Civilians Killed—and Only 2% of a Vital Task Completed." *Iraq Body Count*, May 27, 2003. https://www.iraqbodycount.org/analysis/beyond/100-names.

Smidt, Corwin E. *American Evangelicals Today*. Lanham, MD: Rowman & Littlefield, 2013.

Smietana, Bob. "Many Who Call Themselves Evangelical Don't Actually Hold Evangelical Beliefs." *LifeWay Research*, December 6, 2017. http://lifewayresearch.com/2017/12/06/many-evangelicals-dont-hold-evangelical-beliefs.

Smith, Gregory A. "Among White Evangelicals, Regular Churchgoers Are the Most Supportive of Trump." FactTank: News in the Numbers. *Pew Research Center*, April 26, 2017. http://www.pewresearch.org/fact-tank/2017/04/26/among-white-evangelicals-regular-churchgoers-are-the-most-supportive-of-trump.

Smith, Gregory A., and Jessica Martinez. "How the Faithful Voted: A Preliminary 2016 Analysis." FactTank: News in the Numbers. *Pew Research Center* November 9, 2016. http://www.pewresearch.org/fact-tank/2016/11/09/how-the-faithful-voted-a-preliminary-2016-analysis.

Solnit, Rebecca. *Hope in the Dark: Untold Histories, Wild Possibilities*. 3rd ed. Chicago: Hay- market, 2016.

Spaeth, Ryu. Minutes. *New Republic*, 2015. https://newrepublic.com/minutes/130848/it-terrible-think-left-right-right-years.

Spinoza, Baruch. *Theological-Political Treatise*. Translated by Samuel Shirley. 2nd ed. Indian-apolis: Hackett, 2001.

Stephens, Bret. "Staring at the Conservative Gutter: Donald Trump Gives Credence to the Left's Caricature of Bigoted Conservatives." *Wall Street Journal*, February 29, 2016. https://www.wsj.com/articles/staring-at-the-conservative-gutter-1456791777?cb=logged0.9780561961233616.

Sullivan, Amy. "America's New Religion: Fox Evangelicalism." Opinion. *New York Times*, December 15, 2017. https://www.nytimes.com/2017/12/15/opinion/sunday/war-christmas-evangelicals.html.

Sykes, Charles J. *How the Right Lost Its Mind*. New York: St. Martin's, 2017.

Tacopino, Joe. "Cuomo Deploys National Guard, State Police to Virgin Islands." Metro. *New York*, September 15, 2017, http://nypost.com/2017/09/15/cuomo-deploys-national-guard-state-police-to-virgin-islands.

Taylor, Mark Lewis. *Religion, Politics, and the Christian Right: Post-9/11 Powers and American Empire*. Minneapolis: Fortress, 2005.

Tillich, Paul. *Theology of Culture*. Edited by Robert C. Kimball. New York: Oxford University Press, 1959.

Totenberg, Nina. "Jeff Sessions Previously Denied Judgeship amid Racism Concerns." *NPR*, January 9, 2017. https://www.npr.org/2017/01/09/509001314/jeff-sessions-previously-denied-federal-judgeship-amid-racism-controversy.

Torrey, R. A. *The Person and Work of the Holy Spirit, as Revealed in the Scriptures and in Personal Experience*. New York: Revell, 1910.

Vine, David. "The U.S. Probably Has More Foreign Military Bases Than Any Other People, Nation, or Empire in History." *Nation*, September 14, 2015. https://www.thenation.com/article/the-united-states-probably-has-more-foreign-military-bases-than-any-other-people-nation-or-empire-in-history.

Wallis, Jim. "White American Evangelical Christianity Is a Bubble—And It's about to Burst." *Sojourners,* May 3, 2017. https://sojo.net/articles/white-american-evangelical-christianity-bubble-and-it-s-about-burst.

Washington, James, A., ed. *A Testament of Hope: The Essential Writings and Speeches of Martin Luther King, Jr.* San Francisco: Harper & Row, 1986.

Webber, Robert E. *The Younger Evangelicals: Facing the Challenges of the New World.* Grand Rapids: Baker, 2002.

Williams, Delores S. *Sisters in the Wilderness: The Challenge of Womanist God-Talk.* Maryknoll, NY: Orbis, 1993.

Williams, Joan C. *White Working Class: Overcoming Class Cluelessness in America.* Boston: Harvard Business Review Press, 2017.

Williams, Pete. "AG Sessions Says DOJ to 'Pull Back' on Police Department Civil Rights Suits." *NBC News,* February 28, 2017. https://www.nbcnews.com/news/us-news/ag-sessions-says-trump-administration-pull-back-police-department-civil-n726826.

Williams, Ryan T. "Dangerous Precedent: America's Illegal War in Afghanistan." *University of Pennsylvania Journal of International Economic Law* 32 (2011) 563–613.

Wolin, Sheldon. *Fugitive Democracy, and Other Essays.* Edited by Nicholas Xenos. Princeton: Princeton University Press, 2016.

Wood, Graeme. "His Kampf." *The Atlantic,* June 2017. https://www.theatlantic.com/magazine/archive/2017/06/his-kampf/524505.

Wood, Thomas. "Racism Motivated Trump Voters More Than Authoritarianism." Monkey Cage. *Washington Post,* April 17, 2017. https://www.washingtonpost.com/news/monkey-cage/wp/2017/04/17/racism-motivated-trump-voters-more-than-authoritarianism-or-income-inequality/?utm_term=.6dfc918f98b4.

Wooley, Donald. "Why So Many Evangelicals Support Trump." *The Hill,* March 3, 2017. http://thehill.com/blogs/pundits-blog/religion/322102-why-so-many-evangelicals-support-trump.

Zeal and Ardor (band). "Blood in the River." *Devil Is Fine.* Radicalis Music GmbH under exclusive licence to MVKA Music Limited, 2016 (compact disc).

Zuckerman, Phil. *Living the Secular Life: New Answers to Old Questions.* New York: Penguin, 2014.